I DIDN'T KILL JESUS

The Holocaust, Three Generations

By Naomi Haber

B
Haber
Hab

ISBN: 0615633617
ISBN 13: 9780615633619
Library of Congress Control Number: 2012907431
Createspace, North Charleston, SC

12/9/13

This book is dedicated to my parents
Israel and Inge.
I would like to thank
my sister Hannah, my children Danny, Rebecca and Alex,
and my husband Jon for his continued support,
guidance and love.

FOREWORD

Survivors once had a life before the holocaust.
Children of survivors have lived
with the impact of their parent's suffering all
of their lives. This book was
written for both generations.
-Naomi Haber

CONTENTS

9	Introduction	*Remembering the Past*
13	Chapter 1	*My Father, Israel Offman*
21	Chapter 2	*The Horrors of the Holocaust*
31	Chapter 3	*My Mother's Story*
35	Chapter 4	*After the Holocaust*
37	Chapter 5	*Fighting the War in Israel*
41	Chapter 6	*A Love Story*
59	Chapter 7	*Building a Life*
69	Chapter 8	*Making Sense of It All*
93	Chapter 9	*A New Life in America*
97	Chapter 10	*Another Beginning*
105	Chapter 11	*A Love Story Ends*
115	Chapter 12	*Three Generations*

INTRODUCTION
Remembering the Past

SIX MILLION JEWS DIED DURING THE HOLOCAUST, including one million children. My father's family lived in Poland, and more than 90 percent of that country's three million Jews died in concentration camps, in the ghettos, or on death marches, including his parents, sisters, brothers, aunts, uncles, cousins, nieces, and nephews. Those who survived lived, and still live, with painful memories. Many sleepless nights pass as they relive the horror of their experiences in their dreams. Some are penniless and some have prospered, in countries around the world like Israel, the United States, Germany, and others.

Within the next decade, very few survivors, if any, will be alive. They are the witnesses to and victims of atrocities suffered at the hands of the Nazis. They tell stories of horror, tragedy, and hope. This hope is in spite of the fact that they saw their families murdered simply because of who and what they were.

Jews.

It is enormously upsetting to me, knowing that soon there will be none to tell their stories firsthand—no one to convey the magnitude of the horrors that the human race was capable of perpetrating in Western civilization during modern times.

The story of the Holocaust and the survival of the Jewish people must continue.

My father survived eight concentration camps and lives with the number A1706 tattooed on his left forearm, a symbol of his imprisonment at Auschwitz. The Holocaust occurred over seventy years ago, and the victims, like my father, will soon be gone. They are currently living reminders of a painful, unimaginable past. While my father lived, millions more did not. I grew up without grandparents, and most of my aunts, uncles, and cousins were murdered.

The Holocaust impacts my generation. We are known as the second-generation—sons and daughters raised by survivors. Adolph Hitler, the evil of the twentieth century, put his brand on three generations—my parents', mine, and my childrens'. I don't know what is going to happen to the fourth. People shouldn't forget the Holocaust, and they should learn from history.

There are many children and grandchildren who live with stories of the Holocaust. It wasn't just a story: it was real.

I'm still resentful of what happened to my father.

I was born in 1961 in Germany, and even though I didn't live through the Holocaust, life was more complicated for me, and for others who were second-generation survivors. We were miracles, born to parents who, through fate, made it out alive. I have found that other children of survivors have had experiences similar to mine. We became protectors who had to be close to our parents; and we could not, and still cannot, do anything adventurous in life where our lives might be placed in jeopardy.

This precious first generation lost loved ones, and for the second generation it is unwritten: we must not put our lives in danger, so that we will not be lost to our parents. We think of the pain our parents endured, and we want to protect them. It is a huge responsibility to make our parents happy, and somehow—in ways great or small—we have to make up for the losses they endured. Our parents went through so much hell that they are not capable of any more loss. This is how I felt growing up, and I still feel this way.

My family was always very close. My father rarely spoke directly about the Holocaust, except in little vignettes here and there over the years. But I knew it was because of the hunger and the starvation in the camps that my father insisted our lives revolve around mealtimes for both nourishment and companionship. My parents, two brothers, sister, and I were always together for meals, sitting around our table with vast quantities of food, attempting to replace the closeness of his parents, brothers and sisters, and other relatives who were tragically taken from him when he was just sixteen. We knew our father missed them terribly and thought about them often.

Second-generation survivors, no matter where we lived, often arranged plans of escape, but we were not certain of what we would be escaping from. I once met a woman through a support group for children of Holocaust survivors. She lived in a home with a basement built like a bomb shelter to protect and hide her family from people looking to round them up. Her house was in the suburbs of New York, not in Germany or Poland.

My parents, too, had a plan in the event we had to flee from danger and persecution. One of us would have to leave Germany. I was the designated person, and I did leave eventually—not because of their plan, but because I could not bear being a foreigner, a Jew, in my own country.

The Holocaust affected my siblings as well. We live with claustrophobia and other related issues, as well as many fears. When my two brothers were dating, even before a relationship became serious, their questions to their girlfriends demanded proof of loyalty.

"If someone like Hitler came, would you hide me?" my brothers would ask the young women. "What would you do?"

These are not questions you would typically ask on a date, but for my brothers, the correct answers offered reassurance and settled their anxiety.

The story of my parents, part of what moved me to write this book, is a love story. They met after my father was liberated from his eighth concentration camp and after he had served in the Israeli Army. By conventional thought my mother and father should not have fallen in love and married. Theirs is a love story of a Holocaust survivor and a German woman, living without her parents at the age of fourteen, whose relatives were Nazi sympathizers. Their few relatives were not at all happy about the match. But my parents loved each other, and they married, remaining in Germany for the rest of their lives. My mother converted to Judaism for her husband, and it was she who kept the Jewish traditions alive in our home.

I would like people to learn from the story of my parents. It is so important to remember the past and the lives of people who endured unimaginable and unspeakable horrors. It is important that their stories do not end with them, but continue with subsequent generations.

They continue with me.

CHAPTER 1
My Father, Israel Offman

MY FATHER, ISRAEL OFFMAN, was born in 1925. He has in his possession only one photograph of his family, and it is of his older sister, Faya. This black-and-white photo was taken when she was in her early twenties, a single woman living in Poland with her family, ten years before she was deported to her death in the Treblinka concentration camp. Faya looks very dainty, with small features and pale skin very much like my father's, and long, straight black hair pulled back in a bun. She's smiling at the photographer, who may have been her own father. I don't know what the rest of the family looked like; no photographs survived. I wish there was more to hold on to—anything to serve as mementos of their lives. My father has only his memories.

Possessing just this one photo is such a sad reminder of my relatives who were killed during the Holocaust—people I never met, loved ones my father never saw again, and the grandparents, uncles, aunts, and cousins who were not part of my life. Generations are lost forever. While I treasure the family I have, when I look around the table at gatherings during holidays or weddings, I wish there were more of us. There *should* be more of us.

It was the luck of the draw that my father survived the Holocaust. It was such a horrible, unfathomable experience, with no rhyme or reason as to who lived or died; who was herded to the gas chambers, sent on a death march, forced to work and starve. I grew up hearing stories of the hell people lived through and how they died. I think of these innocent people and wonder, without answers, what did these Jews do to anyone else? And how could the Germans inflict this torture on other human beings?

The victims of this genocide orchestrated by Hitler and the Nazi Party included six million Jews and millions of others, including Romanian Gypsies, Soviet prisoners of war, homosexual men and women, Jehovah's Witnesses and members of other religious groups, and opponents of Hitler and the Nazi regime. The Nazis used the phrase "The Final Solution to the Jewish Question" as they systematically carried out the extermination of the Jewish people from all parts of Europe, including Germany, Poland, Hungary, Czechoslovakia, Greece, the Soviet Union, the Netherlands, Belgium, and Yugoslavia.

My father lived—suffered is probably a better way to describe it—through eight concentration camps from the time he was sixteen until he was twenty. He lost his teenage years to the Nazis and the horrors of the camps, and the memories will always be with him. He talks very little about his experiences. It's much too painful for him, even as a man in his eighties. If and when he speaks about his time in the camps, the memories leave him with nightmares, and he wakes up in the middle of the night screaming and perspiring as he relives his experiences. He never, ever speaks of his family; my family and I know that we must not bring up their names or ask him any questions because he will not answer. Even our questions will cause him to lose sleep.

As a teenager living in Poland, he should have been playing soccer with his friends, attending high school and then college, living with his family, and preparing for marriage, children, and a career in the family business. He was an intelligent young man who could think on his feet, had excellent grades in school, and spoke both Polish and Yiddish. He celebrated his bar mitzvah in the local synagogue, a warm and joyous occasion attended by many relatives and friends. He was small and wiry, with red hair, dimples, a charming smile, and eyes that took in the world around him.

Instead of the fun and typical growing pains of teenage years, and instead of the anticipation of a prosperous future, my father's life became a grueling battle of fear and for survival, with the uncertainty of whether he would be shot, gassed, hanged, or tortured because he was Jewish. And at the end of the Holocaust, if not for a sharp-eyed priest, he would have been buried alive with dead bodies from a local hospital.

My father was born and raised in Czestochowa, Poland, southwest of Warsaw, which has had a Jewish community since 1765. The history of the city itself goes back to 1220. It was, and still is, known as a place where Catholics would gather to worship at the shrine of the Jasna Góra Madonna, the Virgin Mary, so there was very much a Catholic influence and history in that city. A little over 25 percent of the population was Jewish. My father recalls hearing his parents speak about confronting anti-Semitism from the Poles, so life in the town before the Holocaust was not as idyllic as we would imagine.

My father's parents, Raffael and Hanna, were one of the wealthiest couples of the Jewish community of Czestochowa. They owned an oil factory that took up half a block in the middle of the city. Their business employed many members of the Offman family; they processed rape for cooking oil, a staple in every kitchen, and rented out the long basement floor to tenants. They lived not far from the factory in a large home, attended to by a housekeeper and a maid.

Born in 1925, my father was the youngest of seven brothers and sisters living in the house at Stary Rynek 19 (Old Market

Square). He was given the nickname Kucyk, which means pony in Polish. He was a nimble athlete well known for his soccer skills and was in excellent physical shape. His age and physical condition turned out to be major factors in his survival during the Holocaust. His brothers Jacob, Moshe, and Isaac, and sisters Naomi, Tauba, and Faya, were part of a very close-knit family. Mealtimes were especially important for the Offmans, who were religious Jews. They kept a kosher kitchen, observed the Friday evening and Saturday Shabbat and Jewish holidays, and attended services at the local synagogue on Fridays and Saturdays. At home they spoke Yiddish, which is very close to the German language, while speaking Polish outside the home.

It must have been a wonderful experience to live in my father's home at that time. It was a sanctuary, filled with family heirlooms and furniture and the delicious smell of Jewish and Polish delicacies cooking on the stove. In his home, my father, his siblings and their spouses, and often aunts, uncles, and grandparents enjoyed dinner, gatherings, celebrations, and holidays together around the dining room table. Theirs was a very loving and nurturing family, and I could see these qualities by how my father raised his own children many years later.

My grandparents and other Polish Jews had no clue as to what awaited them at the hands of the Germans. News traveled slowly, if at all, and any of the dark, horrible stories must have been met with disbelief. Who could believe what was happening, or imagine that they lived in a world with such hatred and destruction?

Germany invaded Poland on September 1, 1939. Three days later the slaughtering of Jews in Czestochowa began. In what was to be called "Bloody Monday," the Germans began a pogrom based on the false pretense that the Jews of the city had shot at the German soldiers. This was just the beginning of the terror and horror for these innocent people. A mass grave was dug in the middle of the city where the murdered Jews were tossed.

The lives of the Offman family would never be the same again. The killings of Jews and the destruction of their way of life began in the city my father's family had lived in for more than six generations. The Nazis would destroy every iota of the Jewish culture, including the social and cultural structures of Czestochowa.

My father's family and thousands of other Jews were prisoners in their own town. The Nazis set a curfew, which meant that residents were prohibited from being out on the streets between eight in the evening and five in the morning. The Jews were forced to wear Jewish stars on their clothing, which readily identified them. And if they owned businesses, the Nazis stole money and took merchandise without paying for it. Jews were forced into labor and their apartments, businesses, and homes were confiscated. They were robbed and beaten. No radios were permitted, which meant they had no contact with the outside world, isolating them even more. Some were murdered for crimes they did not commit.

As if this weren't enough, the Nazis created a ghetto in Czestochowa and established a Jewish police force within its confines. These Germans knocked on my father's family's door one morning and confiscated the Offman home and factory. The Nazis were going door-to-door and rounding people up.

The Offmans were marched to a neighborhood designated as the "Large Ghetto." Another, the "Small Ghetto," became a slave labor camp. Any infraction of rules meant death. I cannot imagine the fear that hung over their very being. My father was only thirteen years old, and he had celebrated his bar mitzvah just before his family was uprooted.

More than fifty-eight thousand Polish Jews lived in tiny, cramped quarters with little or no space to wash or cook. They suffered and died from cold and hunger; some also died from typhus or other infectious diseases. My father and his brothers wanted to fight back, even though that would mean certain death. They were helpless. He and his family knew that it was only a matter of time before the Germans sent them on a train somewhere. They, and millions of others across Poland and Germany, thought they would be resettled in another town, or even another country. What a lie this turned out to be.

The Offmans lived in the ghetto for three years, and life only got worse. On September 22, 1942, the day after Yom Kippur, one of the holiest days of the year, the Nazis rounded up hundreds of the Jews of Czestochowa and shot them to death in the street. Thankfully, my father and his family were spared, but many of their friends, neighbors, and business associates were not.

My father recalls his mother urging her family one evening, as they sat gathered around their small dinner table in the ghetto, "Eat, eat, you never know when you'll eat again," not knowing how painfully prophetic her words were. It was the last time the Offmans would be together: September 24, 1942. Their futures would be altered beyond belief the following day.

The Nazis began the selection process of who would be sent to the concentration camps by assembling Jews in streets and courtyards. They announced through loudspeakers that the Jews would be deported to work camps in the eastern part of Poland. They said that those who had already been deported were happy and living in good conditions.

What else could these poor men, women, and children believe?

They had nothing. Their clothes were rags, they were starving, and they fought over spoiled food. Many people went voluntarily, filled with hope and thoughts of a happier future. The trains consisted of sixty cattle cars, each filled with over one hundred twenty-five people, with no food or water, light or air.

Seven thousand people thought they were being transported to a better place. Instead, they were sent to their deaths in the gas chambers of Treblinka.

Two days later, more Jews were deported, with a third deportation on Monday, September 28. The fourth deportation took place soon after; these were the Jews who were found in hiding during the first three. The fifth and final deportation occurred on October 4, 1942. The men were sent to Buchenwald and the women to Ravensbrück, and from there they were deported to a number of concentration camps within Germany.

The Large Ghetto of Czestochowa was now empty.

CHAPTER 2
The Horrors of the Holocaust

DURING THE ROUNDUP, my father was separated from his family. He never saw his parents, grandparents, or four of his six siblings again. He was sixteen years old. Because he has extreme difficulty discussing his time in the ghetto and the selection process, some details are limited. He told us that when the Germans demanded his birth date for the selection process, he quickly answered, "May twentieth." He was actually born on July 20, but had learned early on that this was the date an assassination attempt had been made on Hitler's life and that Jews who mentioned this birth date were killed. My father was savvy enough at this young age to have picked up life-saving details that others in his situation often had not.

My father was very sharp, and he watched and listened carefully to what the Nazi SS officers said to each other. Since German is a language very similar to Yiddish, he was able to understand most of what they were saying. He was astute, and he quickly figured out who to stay away from, what to trade for food, how to answer, and who to trust. He learned how to play these games to stay alive.

My father was first sent to Sachsenhausen-Oranienburg, a concentration camp in Oranienburg, Germany, located north of Berlin. This camp, we later discovered, turned out to be the headquarters for the administration of all the concentration camps and served as a training center for SS officers. The camp housed Russian prisoners of war, criminals, Communists, and homosexuals, as well as Jews. Many of these men were executed by shooting and by hanging.

A contingent of prisoners, which included my father, was forced to work in a brick factory. In addition, an airplane manufacturer used labor from Sachsenhausen to support the German war effort. This location also housed a large counterfeiting operation that produced forged American and British currency. Skilled prisoners were brought in from many different camps. These inmates were valuable to the SS, and therefore, received extra food rations. My father remembers how some of these favored inmates shared their food by throwing it out the window.

At this concentration camp, my father, just a seventeen-year-old, watched as the Nazis forced prisoners to perform the "Sachsenhausen salute," a painful position where a prisoner squatted with his arms outstretched in front of him—for hours. Some prisoners would be dangled from posts with their wrists tied behind their back, and if they tried to escape, they would be hung for their crime. Many died from hunger, malnutrition, disease, and pneumonia. My father, largely due to his athletic conditioning as a soccer player, was strong enough to survive.

He was transported to Blizyn, a forced-labor camp in Poland, before he was moved to Auschwitz on a train of cattle cars filled with other men. He did not know where he was headed, whether he would survive the trip, or if he would be sentenced to live or die when he arrived.

"They were all different," my father said of the concentration camps in one of the few times he has ever spoken about his experiences. "But the machinery for death was at Auschwitz."

Auschwitz was the largest of the camps, housing and murdering the most Jewish people. It was patrolled by SS officers with guard dogs, and surrounded by electrified barbed-wire fences. Auschwitz was the centerpiece of the Nazi plan to destroy the Jews and others, and Zyklon B, a cyanide-based poison, was used to murder the men, women, and children after they entered the gas chambers.

My father was assigned to the ramp, which was called *Judenrampe* in German, the first step of the selection process at Auschwitz after the cattle cars were emptied. To be sent to the left at the end of the ramp meant death in the gas chambers; to the right meant one was assigned to slave labor.

"Auschwitz was hell on earth. The worst were the transports from Hungary," my father recalled. "It was so heartbreaking. We were all hardened up. But the Hungarians were so naïve. They had been told that everything would be fine. But we knew that in the first twenty minutes, they would all be gassed.

"Grand rabbis came in clutching Torahs to their hearts, thinking that everything would be fine, that they were going to a safer place. Many of these rabbis became angry toward God and committed suicide by throwing themselves into the electric fences. Every day, death was staring you in the face."

My father's brother, Moshe, once told me that he recalled seeing a grand rebbe urinate on the Bible, look to the heavens and say, "The sky is empty." My only uncle to survive, Moshe was sent to Buchenwald, and it was inconceivable to him and to others that people were being gassed. No one could believe it.

When my father first arrived at Auschwitz, the Nazis wanted to promote him, if you want to call it a promotion, to *kapo*. Had he accepted, he might have received slightly better treatment, more food, and perhaps better living conditions. But my father could not betray his own people by giving orders or beating them, which is what a *kapo* was required to do. My father pointed out his young age of seventeen and suggested that the responsibility should go to an older man. The Nazis, thankfully, decided to choose someone else. They selected a Jew named Pinkas, and he often beat my father. After liberation, Pinkas was put to death by the Polish authorities.

My father, who occupied Bunk 11 in the narrow, cold, barren barracks, described Auschwitz as the most organized of the eight camps he was sent to. Every day, he wished he were one of the German shepherd guard dogs the SS used to guard and attack the prisoners.

"These dogs were treated so well," my father recalled. "I said to myself, 'Why can I not be a dog?' They were well nurtured and well taken care of, and they had enough to eat."

Josef Mengele, known as the Angel of Death, was an SS officer my father saw on a regular basis on the ramp near the cattle cars that brought human cargo to Auschwitz. Mengele would occasionally ask my father to translate orders for him because of Dad's language skills. Life or death meant left or right, and one's future depended on the direction in which Mengele pointed. Their fate was in his hands.

Mengele also conducted cruel and inhumane medical experiments, focusing his intensity on twins, dwarfs, and people with different-colored eyes—or whatever his whim might be at the moment. And when he was finished with mutilating people, he would kill them with lethal injections. My father often stood next to him during his selection process.

"Mengele looked like a movie star," my father said, "wearing shiny black boots and carrying a whip. He sometimes would yell at me to get out of the way, if I was standing on the wrong spot on the ramp. He was looking for twins, and when the trains came in, he was very eager to find them. No one dared ask him what he was doing. But we all knew."

It is difficult, even impossible, for my father to find the right words. There was no respite, no time off or away from these horrors. Instead, the same business of death day after day, of people lined up to be gassed, their corpses piled in mass graves, with their clothing, suitcases, hair, teeth, and shoes organized into piles.

"These terrible moments I have in my mind. It was so bad. It was a helpless feeling. You would see mothers and fathers with their kids, with the little ones held on their chests and holding their hands," he said. "And then they would be dead. People cleared out, with new ones coming in. There were new ones every week."

My father slept wedged in a freezing bunk with other men, his only meal a potato or 123 grams of bread a day, sometimes less. One hundred twenty-three grams is the equivalent of just over four ounces, barely enough to sustain life. He still remembers that amount. Because of the organization of the camp and the speed at which they worked or were killed, there was no time to establish friendships or camaraderie with the other Jews. There was no time to be ill, either.

"I remember working with typhoid and what must have been a hundred-and-four-degree fever. If you said you were sick, that meant a trip to the gas chamber. So I kept working," he recalled.

How he managed to survive Auschwitz and not starve to death is impossible to comprehend. Sometimes he and the other men made a potato soup cooked in the pots they urinated in. He was starving and growing thin while watching older men collapse and die of starvation.

Of Auschwitz, he said, "I saw the most Orthodox Jews give up their faith. They said, 'There is no God, there is no God.'"

Yet somehow my father survived. He recalls a particular day when he was at his assigned job in the crematoriums throwing bodies into the ovens. While he was there, he heard the wives of Nazi officers singing Christmas carols like "Silent Night" off in the distance. As he was returning from his duties, a Nazi officer pushed him into a ditch. My father, using the knowledge he had gathered over the years, instinctively knew that if he did not crawl out of the muddy hole, he would be shot. He crawled out. As he was almost out, the guard pushed him back down. My father was this Nazi's human toy. Up again. Down again. Up again. Down again. This scene played out over and over until the Nazi officer grew tired of the routine. As the guard walked away, he turned, looked at my father, and threw him a pack of cigarettes. They were a valuable gift, for although my father did not smoke, he was able to trade the cigarettes for food.

Hope was not an option. Yet somehow he endured.

"Hope? I didn't have hope," my father said. "Like a creature who just has in mind to get through one day, I just wanted to get through from one day to the next and hopefully get a little more bread or another potato."

My father will tell only a few stories about what he witnessed; they are unbearable.

"I remember one young man who was a singer in the synagogue in our hometown. What a voice. His voice was better than even Plácido Domingo or Luciano Pavarotti," he recalled. "The SS made him sing, and he sang a song by Schumann [the famous German composer Robert Schumann]. He was so excited that he was allowed to sing. A drunk SS officer said, 'That Jew has such a voice. He has to be killed,' and then he shot him. I watched him being killed. I have to live with the memories. *Dante's Inferno* [the first part of Dante Alighieri's epic poem *Divine Comedy*] was a comedy compared to what I saw in my life."

A permanent reminder of Auschwitz is tattooed on my father's left forearm. He was prisoner A1706. But he did not tell me or my brothers and sister what the number represented until we were teenagers.

"My kids asked me, "What is this, Dad?" my father recalled. "I told them, 'This is an old telephone number.' I had so much bitterness and bad memories that I had to overcome, and I didn't want to pass them on to my kids. I wanted them to be happy and to have as much normalcy as possible."

From Auschwitz, my father was transported to Flossenbürg, another concentration camp, this one located in the Bavaria region of Germany and close to the border of Czechoslovakia. Flossenbürg served as a training camp for female guards. More than ninety-six thousand prisoners passed through the camp, with thirty thousand dying there before it was liberated in April 1945. Prisoners were housed in wooden barracks. Flossenbürg also housed a crematorium. Many of the men, like my father, worked in arms factories. Daily executions were the norm, and there were so many bodies to dispose of that they were often soaked in gasoline and set on fire.

My father was then transferred to the Leonberg concentration camp, where most of the inmates worked in the arms business. This camp, like the others, was surrounded by barbed wire and watchtowers, and held prisoners from many European countries. He was in Leonberg for a short period of time until he was transported to Dachau in southwest Germany.

Dachau, the first concentration camp opened in Germany, was divided into two parts: the camp area, where my father occupied Bunk 19, and the crematorium. Its prisoners included members of the clergy who opposed the Nazis, and others who became part of medical experiments.

My father was becoming thinner and thinner and weaker and weaker. He was not certain how long he could survive. There was no end to the horror.

He was transported, for the last time, to Ganacker, a satellite camp of Flossenbürg, in December 1944.

"For every second person, it was the trip of death. We were three days standing in the cattle cars at the train station. At least a hundred thirty people died. The bodies traveled with the living to the camps where they were buried, nameless," my father recalled.

My father's entry form into Dachau.

At Ganacker, inmates were forced to work for Messerschmitt AG, a German aircraft manufacturing corporation known for the bomber planes it supplied to the German army. At this time it was working on a new aircraft, the Messerschmitt Me 262. Inmates were also assigned to enlarge the runway at the camp, even while it was being bombed by American troops every third day. My father said that he and fellow prisoners were not allowed to leave the runway, leaving them exposed while the SS officers hid. At the end of each day, the concentration camp inmates carried off the runway the bodies of the dozen or so that had been killed, ironically, by American bullets.

Conditions at Ganacker were so horrendous that the inmates did not even have bunks, but lived in holes dug in the ground. My father watched as desperate inmates stole food and, as punishment for their crimes, guards turned on garden hoses and forced them down the throats of these poor men until they blew up. He watched as other inmates cut up bodies and removed the livers to eat them. My father recounted this story on German television, one of the few times he ever agreed to be interviewed. He even turned down famed director Steven Spielberg and declined to take part in his Shoah Foundation project to record testimonies of survivors and other witnesses of the Holocaust.

When the US army liberated the Ganacker camp in April 1945, he was skin and bones and close to death from typhoid. He was twenty years old and weighed just sixty-three pounds.

My father was transported to an infirmary in the town of Straubing, which is located in southern Germany. On the way there, he stopped breathing several times. By the time he got to the hospital, he was presumed dead and added to a large pile of dead bodies. A Catholic priest began giving him last rites. My father heard him and opened his eyes.

"Don't," he said. "I'm Jewish."

He lay in his hospital bed surrounded by beds filled with other survivors of concentration camps, all in fragile physical and mental shape. My father watched as some of them, suffering from starvation, stuffed themselves with food and then died a day or two later. With so little food for such a long period of time, the shock to their bodies was lethal. Although he was emaciated and wanted nothing more than food, my father, with the help of the priest, willed himself to eat in moderation, just a little more each day. In the infirmary, the hospital staff treated him like a baby and nurtured him back to life.

My father discovered that his brother Isaac, born in 1915, had starved to death in the Leonberg concentration camp. Isaac and their brother Jacob were also Communists, and were being harassed for this even before the Germans invaded Poland. Jacob attempted to escape from Auschwitz; he was caught and hanged. His sister, Naomi, had given birth to a child, and a cousin had delivered twins. During the selection process, my grandparents each carried one of the twins. The cousin was placed in the line for the labor camp while the others were sent to the line for the gas chambers. But she wanted to be with her children so she moved to the other line. His sister, Faya, was with them. They all died in the Treblinka gas chambers.

From the town of Czestochowa, in all, fifty thousand were killed; eighty-two hundred were liberated.

CHAPTER 3
My Mother's Story

MY MOTHER, INGEBORG MARIE EBENBECK, and her family lived in Straubing, Germany, the town where my father was brought to recover from his years in the concentration camps. Straubing is a small town in the south of Germany with a medieval look where the earliest settlements can be traced back to 6000 BC. It has also had a Jewish presence on and off since 904AD.

The Ebenbecks had lived here for generations, going back to the Middle Ages. They were Catholic, and the family's history in Germany, a cousin of mine once said, went back to the knights. My mother was born on December 13, 1931, in Straubing, to parents who were farmers, and she had a brother, Joseph, and a half sister named Fanny.

Her mother, my grandmother, was Franziska Probst Ebenbeck, and was born in 1896 in Haselbach, a small village near Straubing. For reasons no one knows, she was not to work the farm when she came of age. Instead, her parents decided that she would travel to Munich, where she would train as a maid and then work for a prominent family. In their employ for several years, she became an expert at running a household for the wealthy and, as it turned out, a bit of a snob.

My mother told me that this job taught her mother the importance of how a household was run, from dining etiquette to the correct tablecloth to use, to how to be a gracious hostess to your guests. My grandmother ran her home like a fancy shop no matter how difficult times were. She passed these skills on to my mother, who passed them on to me.

My grandmother's first husband died during World War I. She remarried, only to lose her second husband—my mother's father and my grandfather—in World War II. The marriage between my grandmother and her second husband was more of an arranged union and not a happy one. My grandmother found out that he had a girlfriend, and she felt resigned and resentful.

My mother shared many stories with us about her childhood and memories of war. Her education ended in the eighth grade because she was forced to work to support the family. There was no coal to warm the classrooms, and she spent many hours huddled in bomb shelters. She was often left to fend for herself as a child.

My mother attempted to steal coal, coffee, and food from a nearby US Army base after the war. It turned out that she didn't have to. The American soldiers were generous and kind, and gave her whatever food and candy they could spare. She told me that many times the soldiers gave her chewing gum, and Baby Ruth and Butterfinger candy bars.

My mother and grandmother lived in Heerstrasse, an older part of Straubing. A couple named Kaiser lived in the same building, and my mother was afraid of the husband, a chauffeur for a very high-ranking Nazi officer. She remembered his tall, black, shiny boots and how the heels clicked on the floor. When he entered the building, every resident became quiet immediately, and when my mother heard him coming up the stairs, she would get goose bumps. They all lived in fear of him because saying the wrong thing, innocently or not, meant that the Gestapo could arrest you.

Several of my mother's childhood stories were humorous. She was feisty and never afraid to speak her mind. I remembered this one. She told me that during the war, a kind man tried to make the local children happy by selling homemade ice cream for a penny. It tasted awful, and my mother wasn't shy about telling him so. "This tastes like crap," she informed him.

My mother was part of the League of German Girls, a female branch of the Nazi youth movement. She described it as similar to the Girl Scouts, and during the meetings, they sang German folk songs and were taught survival skills. She gave me a full description of the snug-fitting uniforms they had to wear. Participation in the Hitler Youth was mandatory, and I realize she had no choice, but the fact that she was part of it really nauseated me.

Many years later, I could close my eyes and picture my mother, with braids, a brown shirt, a tie around her neck, singing German folk songs and saluting Hitler. At the same time, my father was imprisoned in concentration camps, standing at the crematoriums, shoveling bodies into the ovens.

Her brother and father were both off fighting in the war. Her brother enlisted in the German Army and fought on the Russian front. Her father, a butcher, made beef jerky for the army and was eventually drafted at the end of World War II. He died in 1945 and is buried in France.

During the war, my mother's brother Joseph was a Russian prisoner and was held captive for many years. After the war ended, he was released from prison and returned to Straubing with a wife.

My Uncle Joseph was tall, dark, and handsome. He had thick black hair that was jelled and combed back. He was much older than my mom. He came to visit once a year around her birthday. My mom and he would sit in the kitchen talking about the old times and the shame Hitler had brought upon Germany. I don't ever remember a smile on his face. I was scared of him, and after a quick hello I would go hide somewhere in the house. I pictured him in a Nazi uniform, and I could not get that image out of my head.

My mother had an illegitimate daughter when she was eighteen years old. Though she later reconciled with her brother, he and his wife, and members of her large family in Straubing, had turned their backs on her when she was pregnant.

My mother was living alone with her young daughter and working as a waitress in a small café. In the town of Straubing, my mother was an embarrassment because her pregnancy was not considered decent. She found a close friend who agreed to raise her daughter.

CHAPTER 4
After the Holocaust

MY UNCLE MOSHE, WHO HAD SURVIVED BUCHENWALD, through a twist of fate, discovered that my father was living in Straubing. My uncle had ended up in Constance, Germany, at the Swiss border, and a man came up to him and said, "There's a guy who looks like you in Straubing. He has the same red hair." On this small lead, Moshe walked for six weeks and arrived at six o'clock one weekday morning. It appeared that everyone in town was asleep until he came across a street cleaner. He asked him if he knew an Israel Offman. The street cleaner said he didn't know anyone with that name. My uncle then mentioned his nickname, Kucyk, and the street cleaner said, "Oh, Kucyk? Why didn't you say so?" The man pointed in the direction where the Jews were living. Off my uncle went, and he found my father.

Their sister, Taube, also survived the Holocaust. She had married a Russian soldier before the war and got out of Poland just in time. She was living in Siberia, and my father reunited with her before she immigrated to the United States. News in the Straubing Jewish community traveled quickly; it was a small community, and people shared information about survivors. He was told that his oldest sister had returned to Poland from Russia. He traveled to Poland to get her and her son, Alex. They returned part of the way by train, through Czechoslovakia and Austria. He crossed over the German border with his sister's child on his back and then they walked the many miles to Straubing.

Life could not go back to what it once was.

"It wasn't easy to live," my father said. "It was a struggle to explain the feelings and the experiences. To be enslaved by the Germans and then try to live again without parents and without families...there were so many tragedies. After people were liberated, so many committed suicide. They couldn't work through their agony. They were so traumatized."

There was no counseling, no psychological support to aid the survivors. While they may have recovered from the physical effects of the Holocaust, the psychological wounds could not be healed. Most of the concentration camp survivors had so much hatred and disgust for Germany that they left as soon as they could. The country and its people were a constant reminder of their torture and pain, and they wanted new lives far, far away. They lived among Germans who were Nazi sympathizers or members of the Nazi Party. In Germany, witnesses to the atrocities, and some participants (willing or unwilling), surrounded them.

But my father took a different path.

He was not a man filled with hate. My father always felt grateful to the doctors and nurses in Straubing who nurtured him back to life. I think that is why he was drawn back to this town over and over again. He knew that the Holocaust, as terrible and tragic as it was, was not the fault of every German he encountered. While he rarely spoke about his past, he thought it was important to move his life forward without bitterness and rancor.

And he did.

CHAPTER 5
Fighting the War in Israel

AFTER HIS RELEASE FROM THE INFIRMARY IN STRAUBING, my father took on a series of odd jobs around the town. As his health improved, he began to catch up on the teenage fun and games he was deprived of for many years. He became an excellent poker player and enjoyed drinking, gambling, the company of different women, and other pleasures many men enjoyed. He earned money smuggling leather goods back and forth between Germany and Poland, making a living this way for several years. When my father grew tired of this, he looked for a more meaningful way for his life to progress.

Although he held an exit visa to immigrate to the United States, he instead chose to fight for Israel. After being humiliated and dehumanized for so long, he felt that now he had a chance to fight back. The Israelis were in the middle of the Arab-Israeli War, already defending their recently formed country.

My father's plan was to enlist in the Israeli Army and return to Germany to marry a girl he had fallen in love with, a Hungarian Jew named Alice, who promised to wait for him. Two years after his liberation from the concentration camps, Israel Offman traveled by train to Marseille, France. While waiting for the ship to take him to Israel, two "ladies" approached him and asked him to come back to their house to meet the madam. This bordello's madam happened to be a survivor of Auschwitz. In an unusual twist, instead of demanding payment for the services of her ladies, when he left the next morning she gave him money for his journey aboard ship to Israel to fight for Israeli independence.

After years of horror at the hands of the Germans, here was his opportunity to fight for the Jewish people. He was twenty-two years old.

"I was so proud that I had this chance," my father said of his enlistment in the Israeli Army. "When I went to Israel, they put me on a kibbutz. I was in the underground, and they gave me the identity of a dead kibbutz member."

My father served in a battalion that included Yitzhak Rabin, who later became prime minister of Israel, and Moshe Dayan, a legendary military leader and politician, in a unit called *Palmach*, an elite fighting force of Jews.

"At first, we didn't have weapons," my father recalled. "With American dollars, we bought rations and weapons. The weapons all had swastikas from the German army. The guns came from Czechoslovakia and were used in the Second World War." How ironic that the guns represented the Third Reich.

He spent a total of two years in the Israeli Army, and was ecstatic when David Ben Gurion, the prime minister of Israel, declared, "We have a state now."

My father returned to Germany in 1950 because of Alice, the Hungarian woman he had met who had promised to wait for him. She was living in Straubing, and he intended to marry her. After they were wed, he planned to travel with her to the United States. But his visa was denied, so he attempted to enlist in the US Army to see if he could gain entrance to the country that way. His brother, Moshe, and sister, Taube, were already living in New York City.

The new state of Israel had offered him a visa for any country but Germany. My father, however, was determined to get back to be with Alice. He traveled by ship to Italy, boarded a train to Milan, and took another train to Salzburg, Austria. He walked over the Alps and crossed the border to enter the German town of Reichenhall. He waited several hours for a train and finally made it to Straubing.

But sadly, after all his travels and hardships while he was away fighting in Israel, when he returned to meet the woman he expected to marry, he discovered that she had married an American lieutenant. After this heartbreaking news, an anti-Semitic official named Mr. Seppenhauser denied him German papers.

So now Israel Offman, a man who had survived eight concentration camps and fought for Israel, was not only alone but stateless. He had no nationality. He tried again to apply for American citizenship, traveling three hours by train to the American Embassy in Munich. This, too, was denied.

"The investigator asked me if I was Jewish," my father recalled. "I said, 'Yes. America gave me liberty from the concentration camps.' He told me no because 'Jews make black market in the Army.'"

My father returned to Straubing and applied for a green card, which he was granted. He was without a homeland, without family and friends, and now, without his intended wife. It amazes me how he had the strength to go on after all this. But he did. When he traveled, he was forced to apply for a visa each and every time. He did have a passport, but it was stamped "Stateless."

The issue of his passport and citizenship became a never-ending saga that lasted for decades. Because he was "stateless," we were not considered German citizens until the mid-1960s, when the German government decided that children would have the same citizenship as their mother.

My father, I think, had mixed feelings about becoming a German citizen. That would have made him official. I'm wondering if he thought, *Why would I want to be a German after all those killings?*

He returned to Poland in 1982 to obtain his birth certificate, as he was trying to apply for his passport again. Sadly, the family home and factory were gone. His birth certificate confirmed that he was born on July 20. My father often said that he celebrated three birthdays—the real date, the fake birth date, and the date he was liberated. He finally received his German passport on October 25, 1986.

CHAPTER 6
A Love Story

ISRAEL OFFMAN'S LIFE AS A JEW IN GERMANY BEGAN AFTER HIS LIBERATION and continued with his return to Germany after serving in the Israeli Army. But with Alice already married, he was feeling lost. He had no family, no structure to his life, and he was uncertain of what the future would be.

Due to a housing shortage in Straubing, it was impossible to find an apartment anywhere. He eventually moved into a little room above the synagogue and went into the business of buying and selling black-market currency, including dollars. Since he was a bachelor with no cooking skills, he ate all his meals at a small café down the block, Café Mariandl. My mother, Ingeborg, wearing her uniform of a black skirt and white blouse, was employed there as a waitress. He enjoyed the typical Bavarian menu, which included potato salad, schnitzel, and sauerkraut, and since he ate there every day, Ingeborg and Israel got to know each other. Soon, she became one of his clients. He sold her dollars and always gave her the best rate.

"Better than anyone else," she used to say.

My mother, with her dark hair and features, was very attractive, even in her uniform. She was twenty-one and my father was twenty-seven. She recalled my father as being smiling and upbeat, with a very good sense of humor. They were attracted to each other immediately. My father was honest with her and said that his goal was to leave Germany. He could not and would not get seriously involved.

My mother told me how much she loved my father and how deeply she felt for all his suffering. She said she loved his humor, and that he enjoyed dancing and gambling and going out to the movies.

"He was making up for his lost youth in the camps," she would say. "He was very romantic."

But most importantly, they both wanted to make something of themselves. I think they both had a feeling of being inadequate. It was like two halves finding their whole, and that was each other.

The relationship of my father and mother blossomed, but it was my mother who became reluctant to continue it. It wasn't that she didn't love him, but because she was German, she felt that no one would accept her marrying a Jew. She knew it was out of the question.

In Straubing, not much was a secret. My parents' relationship was a public one. The Jews who lived in the town were aware of their romance. Many were waiting for exit visas to Israel, the United States, or Canada. Their reaction to my father was, "How can you date a German woman?" My mother always felt the resentment of the Jews against her, and the way Germans felt about her dating a Jewish man.

"There is only one answer," my father said simply. "Love. Love is stronger than anything. Love can do miracles. She said to me, "You can't marry me. I am a German." I said, "Well, I love you."

My parents dated for three years, and my mother moved into my father's little room above the Straubing Synagogue, which many years later became our Hebrew school classroom. At that time, it was unheard of for people to live together before they were married, so this was scandalous.

When my parents spoke of their early lives in that tiny room, they talked about being young and in love. It was their little place. In the corner of the room was a small stove where my mother would cook. There was only room for a bed and a chair. The bathroom in the hallway was shared with a Jewish couple living down the hall. My parents had nothing but shoes and clothing and each other. But when my father, a true romantic, had a little extra money, he brought flowers for my mother. Going through what he did during the Holocaust and meeting such a loving, kind woman gave him a sense of what could be. She made up for his loss of family. She was just beautiful. Before she converted to Judaism, he smuggled a little Christmas tree into the room above the synagogue for her. This story is one of my favorites. It showed me that my father was able to maintain his passion for life. With all the Germans had taken from him, they couldn't take that.

Then my mother became pregnant. She had two options: she could be a single woman with a second illegitimate child, or she and my father could marry. They agreed to marry, and it was her idea to convert to Judaism. She wouldn't have it any other way. My mother began the conversion process with Rabbi Kraus, an Orthodox rabbi from Munich. Not every rabbi was willing to handle the conversion process for a gentile to become a Jew, especially in Germany.

Later I remember Mom talking about her conversion, usually when we went swimming. She had a fear of being under water and could not put her face in the pool or jump from a diving board. Part of an Orthodox conversion requires a visit to the *mikva* (ritual bath). Many preparations need to be made before you enter. Most of them involve intense body cleansing. It also requires two prayers and three full immersions. I can only imagine how hard that was for her to do. My sister was born before the conversion, and my mom was instructed to have Hannah join her. It was obvious to all that my mother was very proud of her conversion. Who would ever imagine that, years later, my mother's proud accomplishment would create a problem for me?

My son Danny was of bar mitzvah age, and we were eagerly waiting for Rabbi Jehuda to call with a date. When he did, our conversation started with a question. "Any conversions in the family?" he asked. "Yes," I answered with confidence. I was excited to share information about my mom's courage and determination to become a Jew. "Well," replied the rabbi, "can we get in touch with the rabbi who performed the conversion? We need some kind of proof of it." Somewhat bewildered, I answered, "Of course. No problem, Rabbi Jehuda." Respecting the rabbi's wishes, I immediately took measures to provide him with the necessary documents. Unfortunately, no matter how many certified and sealed conversion papers I provided Rabbi Jehuda with, none of them were good enough for him. He said that in order to bar mitzvah my son he needed to speak with the rabbi that had converted my mother. Since that rabbi had passed away, this was impossible. The rabbi's solution was to put Danny through a conversion. I got very angry with Rabbi Jehuda. I let him know that his fanaticism was a turnoff to many Jews and that this would hurt his congregation's enrollment—starting with my family and myself. Because he was a rabbi, I held back what I really wanted to say to him. We joined a reformed temple soon after.

My parents were married in Munich on August 18, 1955, by a justice of the peace, as my mother had not yet fully converted. She was eight months pregnant. In a black-and-white photograph taken at the time, my parents look so happy. My father is wearing a dark suit, a white shirt, and a tie, while my mother is wearing a gabardine suit, white shoes, and a little white hat. She is carrying a large handbag and a big bouquet of flowers to conceal her pregnancy. Unless you look closely, it is hard to tell that she is less than a month away from giving birth to my sister, Hannah.

Two Jewish friends served as their witnesses. My parents exchanged simple gold bands with each other's name engraved inside, along with the date of the marriage. This is a tradition that I, as well as my own children, have continued.

My parents had very little money, so they bartered for a crib and other necessities. My mother owned one outfit that she wore until it fell apart. She obtained stockings from American soldiers and followed the rationale that when you get something good, you take care of it. So she had one uniform for work and one outfit for all other occasions. There was no such thing as a washing machine. Undergarments were washed in the sink using a washboard, and a tub was used for washing larger items of clothing. Clothes were hung to dry in their tiny room, alongside the crib.

My mother was such a nurturing and competent woman, and a great homemaker. My father put her on a pedestal.

"She is the best, the next thing to God," he would say.

My sister, Hannah, who was named after our grandmother, was born on September 18, 1955, in a birthing clinic in Straubing. The family remained in that small space with my mother washing Hannah's cloth diapers and hanging them up to dry.

Two years later, in 1957, they were granted a visa to the United States, and flew twenty hours to search for a more prosperous life in New York. My mother had interrupted her conversion to Judaism, a lengthy process, to move to America. My father's brother, Moshe, was living in the Bronx with his wife, Lola, and two sons, Charley and Harvey. His sister Taube first lived in the Bronx and later moved to Brooklyn. There was a factory job waiting for my father, where he worked long hours. He doesn't recall what the workers produced, only that he hated it. My mother remembered that they had a huge apartment the size of a palace and that my sister rode around the kitchen on her bicycle. My parents' apartment was on Bristol Street in Brooklyn.

But my mother still felt like an outsider. She always felt that, among this Jewish family in a Jewish neighborhood with Jewish friends, she was the German. For my father, the Holocaust and the Nazis were behind him. But his relatives did not let him forget.

Sadly, when my father's family met my mother, they were not welcoming, and they referred to her as "the German," as if she were responsible for the conduct of all Germans. She was made to feel like she didn't belong. But she was compassionate. She said she could understand why they would feel that way.

"Can you blame these poor people?" she would say.

When I was a child, my mother would light the Yarzheit candles in remembrance of my father's family, which, according to tradition, must burn for twenty-four hours. We could not even find these candles in Straubing because the only memorial candles were inlaid with crosses. I remember when my mother finally located a gigantic white candle. It was so large that she was afraid she would burn the house down, so she placed it in the bathtub for safety. It was she who insisted on lighting the candles every year.

My parents remained in New York for just less than two years, until my mother became pregnant with my brother, Raffi, who is named after my father's father. At this point, they decided to return to Germany for economic reasons. My father was tired of working in the factory and felt that he could do better in Germany, so they went back to Straubing. My mother returned with my sister on a ship, *The United States*, and my father followed a few months later.

My mother found work as a waitress in a restaurant called the Ring Café. By the time my father joined her in Straubing, the café was for sale. They decided to purchase it, and the building that housed it, with their savings. My father paid sixty-eight thousand

German marks for the building, which would be between thirty thousand and forty thousand dollars today.

My pregnant mother, my father, and my sister moved to an apartment over the café, which was slightly larger than their room above the synagogue. Once settled back into a routine, my mother resumed her conversion to Judaism, and completed the process three months after Raffi was born in 1958. She learned all the Hebrew prayers and said them beautifully. She mastered the art of Jewish cooking from a Jewish woman who taught her to prepare *gefilte* fish, soups, chopped liver, and Passover honey cakes, and she was an expert at baking *challah*. She made her own noodles, too—something my father remembered and loved from his childhood in Poland.

My father turned the café into a nightclub, with dancing, music, and dining, and renamed it Espresso.

I was born in 1961; the third of four children, and my parents lived in the apartment above the café/nightclub until I was three years old.

I was to be named after my father's beloved sister Faya, but a narrow-minded government official refused to allow "foreign"-sounding names. He felt that the Germans would not be able to pronounce them. My father's other murdered sister was Naomi, so my parents named me after her, with the government official only agreeing after they added the middle name of Daniela.

I think back to my parents' marriage, which continued to flourish as their lives evolved in Straubing. They had an immensely supportive relationship. My mother spent her lifetime trying to replace what my father missed from his home and his life in Poland. She helped him cope with the tragedies of the Holocaust by providing him with four children. They were like Adam and Eve—both had no one, and they created this family together to help replace those who were lost.

My mother would comfort my father when he had nightmares about the camps and mourned his lost family. My mother told us about his nightmares so we would not be afraid. They were particularly bad after his cousin in Israel gave him that black-and-white photograph of Faya. It brought back all his repressed agony. My father would wake up screaming and shouting in the middle of the night, and we were all scared. He buried the photograph in a dresser drawer in my parents' bedroom. My mother would take Faya's photo out of the drawer and show it to us after he left the house; she made sure he wasn't around because it was so upsetting to him. Today, Faya's photograph remains hidden in a box, relegated to the closet in a spare bedroom of my father's home.

A LOVE STORY

My aunt Faya and fiancé before the war

Faya's picture was a revelation to us because we didn't know what our father's murdered relatives looked like. I remember staring at her image for a long time.

I learned in a second-generation support group that most survivors will not speak about their lives before the Holocaust. For many of them life began during World War II. With hurt in his eyes, my dad said he had happy memories from before the Holocaust. He recalled a time when, as a child, his parents sent him and his brother Moshe to visit nearby relatives on a Friday before the Sabbath. His uncles, aunts, and cousins were happy to see them. As they entered each house, they were asked, "Did you eat already? How about some food or drink?" Moshe was very shy and bashful, and kept declining, saying, "Yes, we already ate." By the time they got to the third or fourth visit, my dad finally couldn't take it anymore and yelled, "Why do you keep saying we already ate! I am starving and I want to eat, so shut up!"

Once, when my mother was not feeling well, he decided to make soup with potatoes for us. Dad stood over the stove with a smile in his face. With enthusiasm and a big wooden spoon in his hand, he stirred some kind of thick brownish broth in a black cast-iron pot. The smell of the soup was seeping through every room in the house. "Done," he eventually said. We quickly sat down at the kitchen table, and finally got to taste the miracle soup that had kept my father alive in the concentration camp.

"This is what I used to make for myself in Auschwitz, except I used Nazi scraps instead of potatoes. And I cooked it in the piss pots."

A LOVE STORY

My Dad after the war

My Mom at 17.

My parents wedding day August 18th, 1955 in Munich Germany

CHAPTER 7
Building a Life

TURNING THE ESPRESSO CAFÉ INTO A NIGHTCLUB WAS A BRILLIANT DECISION. It was the first club in Lower Bavaria to have rock 'n' roll bands performing live. My father built the café into a very well known rock venue with the help of my mother. Some of her family had been in the restaurant business, and she brought experience and ideas and helped run the club. In fact, I don't think the business would have done nearly as well without her. As it became more and more successful, she began working less, because she had three small children to look after, and then a fourth.

When I was a child, living above the Espresso nightclub was creepy. I was scared to go up to our apartment because of tall, dark stairs that creaked. Some even had holes in them, and I was afraid I would fall right through the staircase. The apartment had more room, and I recall the bathroom with its black-and-white space heater in the middle of it. My mother hated this apartment. She felt that living over a club was not the best environment in which to raise children. We ate downstairs in the club's restaurant.

While my father was auditioning and hiring bands from all over Europe for the club, my mother was in its kitchen, helping prepare the menu and managing the food service. My father would also serve as host, and he was great at schmoozing; he was so popular that people came just to see him. By this time my parents both spoke English, and this appealed to the many US servicemen stationed nearby. Many American soldiers visited Espresso, calling my father Joe. I'm not sure how they came to call him Joe. His name is Israel, and Joe is not even close. They would often place orders for currywurst, a large hot dog topped with curry-flavored ketchup, French fries, my mother's potato salad, and, of course, endless glasses of good German beer.

The club was open from six in the evening to four in the morning, seven days a week and almost 365 days a year. It closed down only for Christmas Day or other religious holidays when dancing was forbidden. To honor his Jewish heritage, my father did not work on Rosh Hashanah or Yom Kippur, but the club was open, and people would line up to hear the bands.

My father was young at heart and was always liked by young people. He had a great ear for music. He knew what appealed to the younger audience, and he created a niche for their music and a hangout for them. My father signed many bands during the sixties, including ones well known today, such as Black Sabbath, the Kinks, and the Scorpions. I love the story of my father approaching Klaus Meine, the lead singer of the Scorpions, and ordering him to "sing" and telling him, "Enough with the screaming."

Business at Espresso was so lucrative that my father opened a second club named Colosseum in the nearby town of Regensburg. At both clubs, bands would practice during the day and perform at night. People came in to listen and to dance.

One of my father's favorite stories is the time he turned down the Beatles. The group wasn't officially the Beatles then, in the early 1960s. He traveled to different places to sign up bands, and in one city, he listened to a group that called itself Tony Sheridan and the Beat Brothers. The Beatles were the backing band for Tony Sheridan, and actually released an album with these members, including him. It was the request for a song called "My Bonnie" by a customer in Brian Epstein's London music store that led their future manager to discover the Beatles. But my father turned them down. He said that he didn't care for their drug use and that he had no patience for self-destructive behavior. The Beatles at that time would play for up to eighteen hours a day and often used amphetamines to keep their energy going. More importantly, my father felt they were too loud for his club, and he didn't want to have to deal with the inevitable complaints, particularly from the church next door.

My father says, "I did the world a favor by not hiring them, or they would have stayed in town and gotten married. The world would never have known who they were." Dad used to say, "I have many marriages on my conscience." He received postcards for many years from couples who had first met in his club.

The hours at the nightclub were very difficult for me as a child because my parents were not home at night. When we came home from school, they would leave for work, and I remember feeling resentful. Weekends and holidays were the most profitable, so they were spent at the club, leaving little time for us.

My parents worked so hard, with long hours, which was rewarding for them because they made a great deal of money. And the more money they made, the more they wanted to work.

We finally outgrew the apartment above the club. We moved to the country in 1965, to a suburb of Straubing after my parents designed a home and had it built for the family. My mother wanted us out of the nightclub environment with its loud music and wanted to raise us in a nice home, something she never had growing up.

We moved to our new home in the village of Alburg when I was five years old. Sitting on an acre of land, the two-story house had five bedrooms, a balcony, and a pool. Our new home was like a villa. It was in a beautiful area surrounded by farms. My father paid cash for the house so he wouldn't have to deal with banks. Dealing with the government, a bank, an agency, or authority of any kind made him fearful. This was an outgrowth of his experiences during the Holocaust.

I loved that house, and have only great memories from there. Hannah and I shared a room, and it had wallpaper, curtains, carpets, and two beautiful beds. The living room was filled with expensive furniture, and the white kitchen had a French door that led to the garden. We all sat on a bench around the kitchen table. We had no housekeeper because my parents didn't trust anyone. My mother assigned chores to us; mine included folding laundry and ironing. We had a pressing machine in the basement, and everything from underwear to napkins was ironed. I also shined shoes. We had no dryer, so clothes were hung up outside in the yard, and if it was raining or snowing, they were hung in the basement.

Along with housing the pressing machine, the basement was home to our pantry. My mother made her own jellies and juices from our cherry, plum, and apple trees. Shopping was done once a month. Food was purchased in large quantities and stored in the basement. There was so much canned food and jellies that sometimes we found it had spoiled by the time we got around to eating it.

My father had a fixation with food. This was a holdover, I think, from the concentration camps and the war. My mother would go shopping in the morning, and my father would go shopping in the afternoon. My father would keep buying food, even when we had plenty in the house. He was obsessed with the freshness of food, as he received only food with maggots in the camps. The freshness gave him comfort. I found out later, when I attended support groups, that many survivors have a fanaticism about food.

We didn't keep kosher, but were holiday Jews who kept the tradition by going to *shul* (synagogue) and services on important high holy days. We ate no bread on Passover. My mother cooked for Purim, Hanukkah, Sukkoth, and Rosh Hashanah, and always dressed us in new clothes for the holidays. This was one tradition from my father's family that we faithfully observed.

Our home was filled with flower-patterned porcelain dishes that my mother loved, particularly the ones produced by a company called Rosenthal, which was popular in Germany and still around today. She loved records, especially operettas, and she liked nice furniture. She made certain that we had candlesticks and Kiddush cups for the Jewish holidays. My parents hung paintings of rabbis, purchased from auctions and exhibits, all over the house. I wonder now if this was because of my father's experiences in Auschwitz, seeing rabbis clutching Torahs and asking where God was as they entered the concentration camp to certain death in the gas chambers. Maybe unconsciously he wanted to show them that there were some who survived.

When the four of us were children, our parents doted on us. They adored us very much, and we meant everything to them. Of course, they had ups and downs and fights, just like in any marriage. My parents never argued over religion; we were Jews and that was that. Business and family kept my parents together. They rarely traveled, as they weren't great at leaving us behind. They had huge trust issues and were afraid that something might happen, that someone would take us away. Traveling and staying away from the nightclubs also put a dent in their business, so they rarely went anywhere.

One time in the 1960s, my parents and Hannah traveled to the United States for the wedding of my father's nephew. Due to visa regulations, once they left the country, they had to spend three weeks abroad. I remember someone staying with us, but it was such a long time for them to be away, and they never did that again.

As a child I remember bringing friends over to visit, but because my father slept during the day and worked in the evenings, we had to be very quiet so as not to awaken him. We swam in the pool and ran around the yard. I have wonderful memories of that house. I felt safe, nurtured, and taken care of, and was shown a great deal of love and warmth.

I was, and still am, close to my siblings. My sister, Hannah, is divorced with two children, Marco and Miriam. She and her significant other, a great guy named Hans, live with my father and care for him. Hannah is the administrator of the Straubing Synagogue. My older brother, Raffi (really Raffael, in honor of my grandfather), was born in 1958. He is now a doctor of geology with his own firm. He lives in Munich with his wife, Evi, and seventeen-year-old daughter, Lea. My younger brother, Bernhard, named after my father's grandfather who was a rabbi, is five years younger than me, born in 1966. A computer scientist who also lives in Munich, Bernhard is married to Karin and has an eighteen-month-old son, Sami.

When we were kids, I remember that Raffi was afraid of the usual childhood things that my sister and I were not. When he was out of the house playing with friends, we would connect thread to his collection of airplane models, tanks, and stuffed animals. We pulled on the threads to lead them out of the room at night. And we attached strings to curtains so they would move. He was always so scared, and he was even afraid to go into the basement alone. I'll never forget those times. He must have hated it, but we had fun.

Bedtime was seven thirty at night, sharp. Once the lights were out, my sister and I would awaken in the middle of the night and pretend we were princesses. We would drape blankets around us, holding them in place with belts and using them as make-believe gowns.

My parents were not the type to read bedtime stories, so Hannah read them to me. My father played soccer with my brothers, and I recall playing Ping-Pong with all of them and the neighborhood boys.

When it came to childhood ailments, my father was extremely attentive when any one of us became ill. I think he was afraid that he would lose us, no matter how minor the illness was. He would come into our bedroom with such a concerned look on his face. When I had the usual childhood rounds of German measles and chicken pox, I was more worried about him because of his anxiety.

He always said, "I wish it were me." And he meant it. The pain of losing his family in Auschwitz, I think, returned when he found himself afraid of losing us.

I remember stepping on a bee once on the terrace, and the pain I saw in his face was greater than mine. When I was attending Hebrew school, I fell and broke my arm and returned home with a cast on it. I tried to hide my cast from his view, as I knew even at this young age how disturbing it was for him to see. He would get so upset. When my younger brother's temperature shot up because of a fever and he lost consciousness, I remember my father running around the neighborhood, screaming for help and looking for a doctor.

We had to consider his feelings more than our own. He couldn't lose anyone else; it was too painful. Once, my mother stepped on a rake and injured her foot, and we had to calm him down. He was so afraid, so fearful that a minor accident would take us away from him forever.

But my favorite memories are of my family, all six of us, together at mealtimes when my mother would cook festive dinners and we would sit at the table, enjoying each other's company and catching up on the day's news and events. This is something I do with my own family, and something my father did with his and always missed.

My parents with Hanni and Raffi in the temple

My first grade school picture at St. Jakobs Elementary school in 1967.
I am in the bottom row 3rd from the right.

CHAPTER 8
Making Sense of It All

ALTHOUGH WE WERE JEWISH AND THERE WERE OTHER JEWS IN TOWN, Straubing had no secular or Jewish schools. So my parents enrolled all four of us in local Catholic schools. My earliest remembrance of school is attending kindergarten in 1965 at St. Jakobs, when I was four years old. A nun named Sister Ritana was very sweet, but one named Sister Bullyfortias was extremely nasty and unkind. I hated going there because she and the other nuns scared me. I lasted maybe two months until my mother pulled me out of class, and then I remained at home until the first grade.

What frightened me most were the outfits the nuns wore. I have vivid memories of the thick white cloth coverings, like hoods, hiding their hair. Over the white fabric were black drapes reaching to the floor. Crosses with metal figures of Jesus were attached to chains and wrapped around their waists, dangling back and forth with every step they took. At that age I barely reached to their waists, and the Jesus figures were at eye level. It seemed like Jesus was in my face at all times. This was quite a frightening picture to a four-year-old. Nuns staring at me while whispering behind my back were the first memory I have of being an outsider. Attending kindergarten wasn't mandatory in Germany. I was glad when my mom took me out.

My parents sent me to Volksschule St. Jakobs when I was six, the school we all attended. My mother accompanied me on my first day of school, and I remember being very nervous. The air smelled of oil from the dark wood floors; I can still smell that grease today. The teachers knew that my family was Jewish because my father was a well-known businessman in town.

I remembered entering the classroom that first day and the large blackboard with a gigantic cross hanging above it catching my eye. Crosses were everywhere in town, so I was familiar with them. My first school day was scary enough—but here I was, looking directly at Jesus on the cross, this poor man, with his head tilted downward. Branches with thorns were wrapped around his head, and blood dripped down his eyes and nose.

Jesus was mentioned in so many prayers, but one in particular stood out. I can still remember the phrase "and the night came upon us and it got darker and darker and it was the Jews who crucified Jesus." I remember how uncomfortable I felt during these prayers, and my blood shot up into the roots of my hair and my face felt hot. The entire class had their eyes on me and gave me dirty looks.

"Please," I wanted to tell them, "don't blame me. I feel sorry for the guy. I had nothing to do with it. I didn't kill him, nor did anyone in my family. I didn't kill Jesus." I could feel everyone's eyes piercing through me.

On that same first day of school, a local newspaper reporter interviewed some of the children. He asked me, "What would you do if you were bullied?"

I replied, "I would make a fist and hit them right in the face. I would beat the hell out of them."

That was my answer; my mother taught me that the first punch is holy. Mom prepared us before our first day of school.

"There is a possibility you'll be going to school with children whose parents were Nazis," she lectured us. "You might get bullied. Make a fist and go right for the nose, but remember: do that only if you get picked on about being Jewish. There is no reasoning with Nazis."

Getting bullied was something I was very fearful of. It made me nervous and cautious in dealing with my peers. Because of this, at times I became a bully myself. In my neighborhood there was a girl I used to play with named Brigitte. She had beautiful, long blonde braids. I had long black hair, and I was not allowed to put it in braids. Mom said it made me look too German. Brigitte knew it and loved waving her beautiful braids in my face, letting me know I couldn't compete with her "Gretel" look. One day I invited her to my house. I don't know what came over me, but I took a pair of scissors and wanted to cut off her braids. My sister walked in the room just in time to stop me. Brigitte left our house crying. I was punished, and her parents wouldn't let me come near their home for a very long time. Another time I pushed a girl named Barbara into a nearby shallow creek, making her believe leeches would eat her up. I believe most bullies act out of fear. I know I did.

During religious lessons, which were part of the curriculum and considered as important as English, German, Latin, or math, I was exempt, so I sat in the back of the classroom and did my homework or drew pictures. My mother had prepared me for this, so I didn't really question it. Sometimes my teachers would offer the religious instruction first and I would arrive later, or they held it at the end of the day so I could leave early. Some were accommodating; others were not.

I don't remember the Holocaust being discussed much in my schooling. If it happened to be mentioned in our studies, it was not discussed in depth. Teachers went over it very quickly in a dismissive fashion.

"Yes, some Jews were killed," was as deep as it got.

While Jews received information and education about the Holocaust from their relatives or at Hebrew school, the Gentiles received almost none. Every so often there was a television program on the subject of the war. I remember as a child of six or seven entering the living room while my father watched a show about the Holocaust. Bulldozers shoveled naked bodies into graves. I couldn't fully comprehend what I was seeing.

"Get out of the room," my father ordered, and I complied. These images stayed embedded in my brain for a long time. Years later I found out he was watching "Night and Fog", a French documentary made about the holocaust 10 years after the war.

Now, I wonder how he was able to sit through it. I was in shock. This was the first time I began to understand what evil was. I started asking questions and learned more about the Holocaust from my mother and siblings. Today there are many television documentaries, movies, school and museum programs; back then there were very few. Straubing chose to ignore the Holocaust for many years. In 2010, when I visited the Straubing Museum, which preserves the history of the city and holds a celebration every year, I noticed a glaring omission: when it came to the years during World War II, there were pictures of the local festival and other events, but no mention of the Holocaust or the Jews. It was as if we hadn't existed, and the destruction of cities and murders of millions had never occurred.

In school, Hanukkah and other Jewish holidays were never mentioned; most children were unaware of Jewish customs and celebrations. German children were curious, and would ask me questions like, "Why don't you celebrate Christmas?" Or, "Why don't you celebrate Easter?" These are very normal questions for children to ask, but I was a child myself, and sometimes it felt like they were attacking me. But looking back now, they were just curious.

I often felt left out. German children celebrated Easter and Christmas and attended mass on Sundays. And at Christmas, Santa Claus would visit our school, dressed in a long golden gown with a large matching hat. He had a white beard, black boots, and a huge walking stick, and he carried a large sack of gifts. He brought gifts for everyone except me. One of my teachers, Mrs. Moser from the first grade, was very kind, and she included me when the rest of the class received nuts and tangerines. The first time Santa Claus came to Mrs. Moser's class, I was scared. I had never seen anything like him before. Excitedly but cautiously, I accepted Santa's gift. I didn't eat the tangerines and nuts, but that particular day I felt equal.

Being the only Jew in my class could be an uncomfortable and isolating experience. I continued to feel like an outsider. My friend Monica made me feel less lonely when I was in elementary school. Monica's beautiful, shiny blonde hair came along with a sweet, bubbly personality. I was invited to her home many times, and her parents were just as kind as she was. Christmastime in her house stands out the most. The smell of freshly baked cookies and the festive decorations, which included a gigantic Christmas tree with stars and silver tinsel hanging from the branches, made me not want to leave her home. I couldn't take my eyes off the display under the tree: Joseph, Mary, and the three wise men bringing gifts to Baby Jesus. It looked so calm and beautiful. During Christmas I resented being Jewish. I wanted to get lots of presents, but most of all I wanted to embrace Jesus and be allowed to believe in him. Monica's mom must have picked up on my dilemma and always had a gift under the tree for me. Thinking back, I know now why my mom was melancholic during Christmastime. She missed this beautiful holiday.

When I was twelve or thirteen and walking home from school with a young boy, we were talking about Christians and Jews.

The boy said to me, "You know, Naomi, you're only half-Jewish. Your mother was not born Jewish. Your mother converted."

"That may very well be," I retorted. "But I feel like a one-hundred-percent Jew, and I'm proud of it."

He said, "OK," and looked at me, bewildered.

It was beyond his comprehension.

Each school I attended permitted me to take off from class to celebrate the Jewish high holidays, including Rosh Hashanah and Yom Kippur. When I returned to school, my classmates wanted to know where I had been. I felt that they were looking for reasons to make me feel different, and I found this attitude condescending.

While the other kids did not make fun of me or bully me, their looks really bothered me. Time-wise, this was more than twenty years after World War II, and it was and still is forbidden to make any anti-Semitic remarks. A violation of this German rule would mean a large monetary fine or six months in jail, so parents may have warned their children not to say anything.

I was a pretty little girl and dressed very nicely, and I spoke the Bavarian dialect like the others. In this respect I fit in easily. My mother grew up in Straubing and her family went back many, many generations. There were a few other second-generation Jewish children in Straubing, but they fit in even less because they couldn't master the Bavarian dialect. I shunned them. I did not really want to socialize with Jewish children. They were too intense for me and too segregated from German society. I didn't want that.

As a child, I could tell how teachers felt about me. A good student, I knew that with a decent teacher, my grades would be better; with an anti-Semitic one, my grades would be worse.

My third grade teacher stood out in a most positive way. His name was Mr. Avril, and I blossomed in his class. I recall being one of the better students because he was so nice and kind. That made all the difference. He also told the class that it was Pontius Pilate who killed Jesus. So for at least one year, I was off the hook.

Knowing that I was one of Mr. Avril's favorite students made me feel stronger and more confident. I remember Easter approaching that year, and the class was busy preparing for the holiday. Painting Easter eggs was great fun. But I painted landscapes instead. There was a buzz going around the classroom: the holy priest was arriving and would give special blessings to all the kids in class to prepare them for Holy Communion. I remember him walking in, and instantly, every child rose from his or her desk to make the sign of the cross. I stood, as usual, with my hands at my sides. The holy priest, Father Resch, smiled as he greeted the children. He asked them to come up to the front of the room. The kids quickly lined up with their mouths open. Father Resch made a cross in the air in front of each one, said a prayer under his breath, and put a wafer on every child's tongue.

I remember feeling envious of my female classmates. I knew what they would get to wear when the big day arrived. They would look like little brides. With white lace dresses, shiny white shoes, and beautiful veils covering their faces. They would hold tall candles with lace attached and white little Bibles that they would proudly march with.

Father Resch noticed me in the back of the room and called out, "Naomi, I'll be happy to give you a blessing as well! Come, my child. No harm will be done to you."

That was one of the moments I wished the earth would open up and swallow me. On the one hand, I so wanted to please this very nice priest who had a warm and friendly smile. On the other hand, I knew that if my parents ever found out that I had taken a blessing from a Catholic priest, all hell would break loose. So, I respectfully declined his blessing.

Later that day, a classmate asked me, "Is it true that Jews cut up babies during the Jewish Easter holiday and drink their blood?"

I became so angry that I shouted at her, "Yes, it's true, and if you don't piss off, I'll eat you!"

The girl was in shock and ran away. I felt bad about what I said and told Mr. Avril about the incident. He knew just how to handle it.

"I have an idea," he said. "Tomorrow when you come to school, we'll talk about the Jewish Easter, Passover. Is there anything you could bring to school for the kids to see and learn about your holiday?"

I was so excited. My mother gave me a box of matzo to take to school. All the kids were amazed and curious. They had never seen anything like it and asked so many questions.

"What does it taste like?"

"What does it smell like?"

"Is that the kind of bread God let rain in the desert?"

As the kids ate the matzos, I explained more about the Passover holiday. I educated them.

"You have an Easter hunt and look for eggs; we hide matzos," I explained.

My classmates were really interested and kept asking more questions.

"So, how do you Jews celebrate Christmas?"

"Well," I replied, "we call it Hanukkah, the Festival of Lights. It is really similar to Christmas. You light Christmas trees. We light menorahs. So you see, it's not so different after all."

I became everyone's best friend that day.

I came to realize that it is fear of the unknown that can make children aggressive and turn them into bullies.

A great deal of thanks goes to Mr. Avril. This story shows what a difference a teacher can make in the life of a child. I have never forgotten him or his kindness.

But in the fourth grade, my experience was completely different. My teacher often hit my classmates, and if they gave a wrong answer, she smacked them on the hand with a ruler. She made me very nervous, though she never hit me. I was afraid of her. She often referred to me as an Israelite

We started learning English in the fifth grade, and it was my favorite subject. I loved the sound of the words, and I was very good at it. I felt like I was born to speak English.

At the same time I began public school, my parents also enrolled me in Hebrew school. The teacher, Mr. Rosenfeld, was the smartest man I'd ever met. There were six of us, all different ages thrown in together. When our twice-weekly Hebrew studies were finished, he would then tutor us on other topics such as Algebra, Latin or economics.

Our Hebrew class took place in the Straubing Synagogue, in the same room that my parents once lived in. It was turned into a classroom, filled with benches and a blackboard. I couldn't picture how my parents had lived in this small room, but somehow they had managed. Mr. Rosenfeld would sit in his chair, teach us Hebrew reading and writing, and prepare the boys for bar mitzvahs. Because I was exempt from the religion class in public school, my Hebrew grades counted on my report card.

While our brothers each had a bar mitzvah, complete with the religious service and celebration afterward, Hannah and I had nothing. In my parents' generation, girls were not considered as important as boys, so this coming-of-age ritual was not a priority for girls. The preparation for my brothers' bar mitzvahs was not an easy task. Their parties took place in the community room of the shul. This meant that the food and beverages had to be strictly kosher. There were no kosher butcheries in Straubing. No kosher caterers. So the goods had to be brought in from Frankfurt, which was a four-hour car ride. Wines had to be shipped from Israel. When the foods finally arrived, it was my mother, sister, and I who had to cook and prepare for one hundred fifty people. It was a lot of cutting, stirring, and mixing. My mom was an excellent cook, and her personal touch made everything taste delicious. Dad hired a band, and there was dancing and singing. We had lots of fun, which made the cleanup the next day so much easier. It was hard to believe that only twenty-five years earlier, the Germans had almost succeeded in burning down our synagogue.

Instead of a bat mitzvah, when I was fifteen, I received a trip to America. My father took Bernard and me, and we stayed with Aunt Taube in Brooklyn. Taube's husband, Aaron, had died in Russia while serving in the army fighting against the Germans, and left her a widow with one son, Alex. She had remarried a man named Paul, and she invited us to visit. Paul introduced me to the most delicious food: bagels and cream cheese.

I fell in love with the United States. I loved how nice the Americans were. People were so friendly. And Uncle Moshe and his family took me to the Statue of Liberty, the New York Botanical Gardens, and the Empire State Building. It was the first time I had seen skyscrapers, except in the movies. This was such a great trip, and it left a tremendous impression on me. I was among so many Jewish people, and I felt free, not like I was walking on eggshells as I did in Germany.

"I could move here. Get me out of Germany. I would like to live here," I told my father.

But first, I had to complete my education.

School lasted from eight in the morning until one in the afternoon. After the fifth grade, you were forced to make a decision about your path in life and select the most suitable school. It was too early to make a decision like this, but that was how the German educational system operated. My parents wanted me to learn business skills so I could do whatever was needed to benefit the family, even though I was not interested in business. I just wanted to make it through school. I really didn't want a future in Germany.

My parents hoped that if I obtained a business degree, they could use me in the nightclubs, handling typing, stenography, and administration. But it wasn't what I wanted. Growing up in such an old-fashioned family, it didn't matter what the girls wanted to do, so I went along with the plan and enrolled in a school specializing in business. I attended Pindl Business and Commercial School in Straubing from 1973 to 1977.

Some of my classmates were sons and daughters of the SS members and of Nazi sympathizers. In retrospect, this is chilling. At six years old, all I knew was that I was Jewish. I didn't know about the SS. When I was in ninth grade, one of my close friends, Dona, confided in me that her father had been a member of the SS. Her confession cut me like a dagger. I was a regular visitor in her home and had shared many meals with her parents. The thought of sitting at the same table with a Nazi made my stomach turn. Dona was ashamed of her father's history. I explained to her that she had nothing to do with it and that I wanted to continue our friendship. I made it clear, however, that I would never set foot in her house again. She respected my decision.

I had another close friend, Victoria, whose home I would often visit. But I was not allowed there when her grandmother came over because she was a fanatical anti-Semite. My girlfriend used to warn me, "Naomi, get out. She is on her way!"

One day, however, Victoria's grandmother decided to pay a surprise visit. We were in the middle of a game of checkers when the doorbell rang. We ran to open the door, and there she stood, the grandmother I had to avoid at all costs because she hated Jews. I needed to make a quick getaway. She was a big, scary-looking woman with many wrinkles and oversized yellow teeth. She was leaning on her cane, looking at me through her large eyeglasses. My knees got soft, standing in front of the monster woman.

"You need to go home now. You are not welcome here," she said.

I ran as fast as I could out of the house. Still shaking with fear, I walked past my house several times. I decided that no one should realize what had just happened. Being kicked out of my best friend's house was humiliating. What did I do to make that woman hate me so much? She probably thought I had something to do with killing Jesus. That had to be the reason. I wanted answers. Who killed him? And why? I needed to find out.

I must have been twelve or thirteen when I approached my dad with the question that had been haunting me for a long time. "Dad," I carefully whispered, "please tell me—did the Jewish people kill Jesus?"

He looked at me with a smile and answered, "Well, Naomi, first off, you need to know that Jesus was Jewish. He was a scholar and a very wise man. This is what we Jews believe. Christians believe that Jesus was born in Bethlehem to Mary and is the Son of God. What we know for sure is that Jesus was a very good man and helped many people. Jesus lived during a very troubling time. Many young people loved him. They followed him and listened to his lectures on how to be good to each other. At the same time, he made many enemies because people got jealous and didn't like his success. Jesus became more and more powerful and got in the way of the Romans, who were ruling at the time. Rabbis also felt threatened by him. Some bad people got together and decided to get Jesus out of the way. Because Jesus was crucified in the land of the Jews, we got blamed for his death. Even though so many people of other religions were joining in, nobody wanted to take responsibility for it."

During my high school years, I had good friends, and I still remember Gabi, Cornelia, Doris, Uschi, Ernie, Harold, Thomas, and Armin, but I didn't know anything about their parents.

I don't remember studying or learning about the Holocaust in high school, and when World War II was mentioned, pages in textbooks were turned very quickly. In the tenth grade, my class visited a concentration camp in Austria named Mauthausen. The principal, Mr. Pauli, thought it might be an interesting addition to the field trip we were making from Straubing to Vienna. I walked into the concentration camp with my classmates. Within ten minutes I became upset after looking at photographs depicting the camp and its inmates.

This visit to Mauthausen was not initially part of the trip itinerary, so when Mr. Pauli made the announcement, I knew my exciting class trip was about to end.

I remember walking through the gate, with the sound of the gravel under my feet pounding in my ears. It was late in the fall, and a bone-chilling wind blew through the camp. For a moment, I thought I heard crying and screaming. Was it the wind making the noise?

I followed my classmates into a building. It had been made into a museum, with many photographs of Jews wearing striped outfits resembling pajamas. Emaciated women, men, and children with sunken eyes stared at me. I walked through the rooms filled with photographs of more horror and sadness.

Was the old man with a beard my grandfather?

Was the young woman holding on to her child my aunt?

Was the young man lying dead on the ground my uncle?

Was the little boy looking out of a tiny hole from a cattle car my dad?

My knees felt weak. I found it hard to breathe. All of a sudden, tears began rolling down my face. The room became smaller and smaller and smaller. I couldn't stay there a minute longer. I ran out of the building gasping for air, and climbed back on the bus. I buried my face between my knees, sobbing. My classmates returned, laughing and giggling. My girlfriend Uschi sat next to me and gave me a big hug. She cried with me.

A stoned-faced Mr. Pauli made an announcement on the bus microphone.

"Everyone. Please. What you saw was exaggerated and a bit blown out of proportion."

I was livid. I got up from my seat and yelled, "How can you say that? How about asking my dad!"

He replied, "Well, it's only pictures." He patted me on the head like a dog. "I know you're affected by this, Naomi."

He must have been a leftover Nazi was the only conclusion I could reach.

When I told my parents, my mother said, "Well, that's to be expected."

And my father offered the explanation, "Maybe he was trying to save the day." He did not want to see me upset, so he tried to smooth it over.

But I was angry at the principal's insensitivity and confronted my father.

"How could you settle in a country that did such harm to you?" I asked angrily.

"Not all Germans were bad," he replied in his usual manner.

My father's understanding and forgiveness were really on display when my older brother Raffi introduced his new girlfriend, Gertrude, to my parents. This was at the same time that I was confronting anti-Semitism in my school. As it turned out, Gertrude was the granddaughter of Fritz Saukel, a Nazi war criminal who was hung during the Nuremberg trials. He had worked directly under Hitler, managing the enslavement of millions from the lands that Germany had conquered. I remember my brother bringing her to our home only once. Ironically, it was my mother who was upset and yelled at my brother, ordering him never to let her set foot in our house. My father tried to defuse the situation by saying, "She is a child, and not to be blamed for her grandfather's evil crimes." My father gave my brother his blessing to continue dating her. My mother, on the other hand, stood her ground and let it be known that she was not fine with it.

I remember looking at this most beautiful girl standing in my parent's front yard. Her long brown hair reached down to her hips. How could someone so lovely have such a monster of a grandfather? The tension became untenable, largely because of my mother's strong disapproval. The romance ended soon after.

Years later I asked my brother what he was thinking at the time. And his answer was, "Like a typical teenager, I wasn't."

Later that year, the principal retired, and we had a new principal named Mr. Bovik for the following school year. He must not have known that there was a Jewish student in the school. I was in the tenth grade, and my class was waiting for a substitute teacher. We were running around chasing each other, throwing paper balls and creating a general ruckus. Mr. Bovik came in and admonished us.

"You stop behaving like they behave in Jewish schools," he warned us.

My girlfriend asked me incredulously, "Did you hear what he just said?"

Then he said it again, and added, "You act like stupid Jews."

I was furious and followed him out of the classroom. He turned around.

"What are you doing outside the classroom?" he asked me.

"Did you make a comment about stupid Jews?" I demanded.

Mr. Bovik admitted that he had and turned beet red. I knew that what he had just said was in violation of German laws, and by his obvious sweating, so did he. He must have been a member of the SS or Gestapo during the war. I exposed an anti-Semite! I had a chance to get back at someone whose beliefs had caused so much misery in the world. Revenge was racing through my head. I must admit, I felt empowered. I could take it as far as getting him fired. What I really wanted to do was put him in a striped outfit and stick him in a concentration camp. I was and still am a firm believer of an eye for an eye, a tooth for a tooth.

"I'm a Jew," I responded angrily. "I'm going home to tell my parents, and the newspaper would like to hear about this, too."

Mr. Bovik apologized. "You may have an inferiority complex about being Jewish," he told me, attempting to make this my problem. "I apologize," he said. "I won't say it again."

My parents' reaction was upsetting: they didn't want to rock the boat. But I was ready to fight and speak to the newspapers. This was not something my siblings would ever have done.

My parents said, "You're almost done with school."

I was disappointed with their reaction.

At what point are you going to stand up? I thought. This principal's feeling was that, as a Jew, you shouldn't be living in Germany. And I hated that.

My parents did not write a letter to complain, and they told me, "You either continue school and live with it, or we'll take you out of the school."

The school wasn't going to fire Mr. Bovik unless I really pushed for it, and my parents felt that by the time this happened, I would have graduated.

I did one thing after this incident. My father had given me a gift of a Star of David on a necklace from a previous trip to Israel. It was so large that it covered most of my neck. I wore it to school from that day on, to let Mr. Bovik and the rest of them know that Jews had a voice.

I made sure that many people heard about his comments, and I told other teachers that they were dealing with an anti-Semite. He resigned a year later. I'm not sure if my complaints had anything to do with his resignation, but I was happy to see him go.

From this experience and others, I learned that no matter where I am, I am going to have to deal with this anti-Semitism, by toughening up, talking back, and standing up for myself.

My parents did not nurture a social life for themselves or for their children. They would not allow us to participate in after-school activities like the Girl Scouts or sports programs. They wanted us home and sitting together at the dinner table. My parents found that when they socialized with Germans, they would eventually insult Jews, and if they socialized with Jews, they would insult my mother because she was German.

But my parents did one great thing that really became my foundation and offered me self-confidence. At the recommendation of Mr. Rosenfeld, the Hebrew teacher, they sent me to summer camp. Mr. Rosenfeld suggested it so that I could meet and interact with other Jewish children. Every year I asked my parents to send me there, and they did. It was so beautiful, and I lost all my anxieties and worries about being Jewish. You didn't have to look around to see who was listening when you used the word *Jew*. We had six weeks of summer vacation, and I spent three weeks in a summer camp run by a Jewish organization. Each summer meant three glorious weeks in a different city or location in Germany, including camping in the famed Black Forest.

Many of the counselors came from Israel. They introduced me to Israeli songs and folk dances. Friday evenings were the most special. I remember them preparing beautiful Sabbath meals adorned with fancy China and large candles. They were always talking about Israel with such enthusiasm and tried to convince us to visit there. A tremendous feeling of comfort came over me at that time.

When I was in high school, I decided that I wanted to move to Israel. I refused to live in Germany. I informed my parents, "I'm done with Germany. I feel that as a Jew, I cannot live here. It is my duty as a Jew to live in Israel."

At first, my parents thought I was joking. But I was very rebellious, and threatened to lock myself in my room and not come out. I hated living in Germany, and I meant what I said. After some convincing, they became open to the idea and thought of it through the survivor's mentality: I could pave the way if the rest of the family had to get out of Germany.

I handled the details myself and contacted the representative in charge of an organization that helped German-Jewish kids immigrate to Israel. His name was Micha Feldman and later in life he became a major figure in bringing Ethiopian Jews to Israel. I took care of the paperwork and met with the agency's representative in a coffee shop. He wanted to know why I desired to move to Israel. I told him that it was a good decision for me and that I would be free of all the anxieties I had about living in Germany. Israel would be like home to me. He got the ball rolling. The only issue was that I had to be eighteen years of age. I lied and told him that I was eighteen—that I had lost my passport and would submit my paperwork later.

My suitcases were packed with my clothes, my cassette tape recorder, and my favorite music. I had so many suitcases. Most of my personal possessions were packed because I had no intention of coming back to Germany. This chapter of my life would be closed.

My father and I flew to Israel. I was sixteen years old. There is a sweet smell to Israel, which hit me as soon as I took my first step off the plane. Happy and confident, I was ready to begin a new future in the Holy Land.

My father was the one to escort me because he spoke some Hebrew, so he was more comfortable going with me than my mother. I remember that we took an early morning flight, and my mother hugged and kissed me good-bye, wishing me all the best. I think she thought this was a crazy teenage thing and that I would be back in a couple of weeks.

"Take good care of yourself and stay out of trouble," she advised me.

My father and I arrived in Israel. The agency representative, who had taken my word for it that I was eighteen, arranged for me to live on a kibbutz. My father had cousins living in Israel, and he felt more secure knowing that I had some sort of safety net in the event I needed a helping hand or had an emergency. He contacted my cousin Tzuria, a single woman in her thirties, and we stayed with her in Tel Aviv before settling me in.

There was something I felt I needed to take care of before I moved to the kibbutz. While my dad was visiting a friend in Tel Aviv, I decided to take a bus to Jerusalem. I needed to get to the Church of the Holy Sepulchre, located in the Old City. Clueless on how to get around, I took a taxi right from the central bus station to the church. It wasn't a particular vacation time or holiday so the crowd wasn't too bad. The intense smell of incense hit me as I entered the church. I saw Greek Orthodox priests gently swinging smoky thuribles back and forth while they were saying prayers. Further into the church was the Altar of the Crucifixion, where Jesus was crucified. Men and women from all over the world lined up to see where Jesus died. I was one of them. With tears rolling down their faces, people said prayers. Finally it was my turn to stand in front of the altar in the very same spot Jesus was killed thousands of years ago. It was dark and yet so bright. There were candles burning, Madonnas with shiny diamonds in their crowns, and flowers all around. Incredibly beautiful. It didn't matter what religion you followed—being there was an indescribable experience. Being Jewish, I didn't feel right praying to Jesus, but if there was any chance Jesus could really hear what people were saying, I didn't want to get blamed for his death anymore. I thought to myself that I would have been a fan of his had I lived during his time.

My father dropped me off at the kibbutz. The room I stayed in resembled a run-down shack with paint peeling off the walls. He had very mixed feelings about leaving me alone there.

I could read his face: *Are you sure you don't want to come back with me?*

But I was absolutely certain that this was what I wanted.

"This is where you want to stay?" my father asked, sounding surprised when he entered my little hut that looked more like a prison cell with a metal bed in it.

The kibbutz accommodations were far different from what I was used to in Germany. Kibbutzim, at least back then in the '70s, were looked upon as a utopian society, where people lived a communal lifestyle with few possessions, and they shared work responsibilities. Men and women shared the same tasks in the fields on rural lands, and they all worked together to preserve the land and culture of Israel. It was very primitive, and my father could not understand why I would want to live like this. To him, it must have looked like I was going backward and giving up all he had worked so hard for. But I was determined to live in Israel.

"I'm making my life in Israel," I informed my father, and I said good-bye.

He returned to Germany to my mother, brothers, sister, and his nightclubs, and I began working in the Kibbutz Geva that December with the intent of making *aliyah (immigration to Israel)* and becoming an Israeli citizen.

At the kibbutz, I was required to work six days a week. I was scheduled to work four hours in the morning and study Hebrew for three hours in the afternoon. I really loved life there, and ended up staying for six months. Geva was founded in 1922. There were approximately one thousand members during my stay. The day was extremely regimented while we worked to earn food and housing. My assignment was to pick grapefruit, something I knew absolutely nothing about. We met at five thirty a.m. in the kibbutz's dining room hall. Flatbed tractors arrived first thing in the morning. We hopped on and then worked in the fields putting grapefruits into buckets. This was hard work, and included crouching on all fours to pick up grapefruits on the ground that had fallen from trees. If the grapefruits were still on the trees, I maneuvered a heavy ladder under the trees and climbed to pick them. There's a certain way to twist grapefruits from trees, and it was not easy. My back and arms were in pain, and I worried about snakes and spiders. In the kibbutz, each person had an assigned function. Some worked in the factory that made machine parts, while others, like myself, did the fieldwork. I picked grapefruits for two long months, from five thirty until nine thirty in the morning, and then I was permitted to rest, freshen up, and eat a snack.

I picked so many grapefruits that I even did it in my dreams. They were so sweet and delicious. We also picked olives from little bushes and walnuts from trees.

Socially, the kibbutz was wonderful, and it was interesting to meet people from every continent. In the evening, we would meet at these clubs on the kibbutz, serve hot chocolate, play board games, and get to know one another. I spoke "school" English and so communicated with everyone in English. There were two programs offered: one was half work and half school and the other was all work. I was in the former.

After two months of picking grapefruits, I was reassigned, thankfully, to the children's house, which consisted of watching ten to twelve-year-old children of kibbutz members. This was a more prestigious position. The day also began at five thirty a.m., when we prepared a breakfast of scrambled eggs, salad, and French toast, and served it at six. My partner in the children's house was a woman from Manhattan named Sari Koch. She prepared the eggs and French toast, and I made the Israeli salad, which consisted of tomatoes and cucumbers. Once the children ate breakfast, we would clean the kitchen and the bathrooms. I had such a love and passion for Israel that I would have done anything.

While my teachers, textbooks, and parents in Germany had said little about the Holocaust, it was a common subject in Israel. For the first time in my life, I felt safe. I felt comfortable talking about the Holocaust. In Germany, if I brought it up, people became hostile or uncomfortable. In Israel it seemed that everyone had some sort of relative who had either survived or perished in the Holocaust.

Strangely, there were non-Jewish Germans serving in the kibbutz. Because Jews surrounded me, I felt powerful. I felt superior to these Germans and thought that perhaps they were there out of guilt. I wanted to tell them that they had no business being there, but the kibbutz was open to all, and it was not my place to condemn them.

I remember shopping at a concession stand in Tel Aviv and overhearing the elderly couple who owned it conversing in

German. I noticed that they had inmate numbers tattooed on their left forearms, so I knew they were survivors. As they continued talking, I thought, *My God! Someone speaking my language!*

I asked for a soda in German, and they closed the shutters to their shop in my face. They thought I was German, and couldn't comprehend the possibility that a young Jew from Germany could be living in Israel.

As time went by, I was starting to feel out of place in Israel due to constant questions about my heritage. The questions made me feel frustrated and alone, isolated and homeless.

Is there a place for me in life? I questioned. *In Israel, I am a German to these people, and in Germany, I am the Jewish one.*

Telling my story of being a German Jew was wearing me out and frustrating me. I felt I should not have to explain my situation everywhere I went. I started to tell people that I was from Switzerland to avoid their looks and questions.

After six months, the kibbutz lifestyle became much too routine and monotonous for me. I also found that when you live in a close community, there's a great deal of gossiping, and it started to get to me. It was time to make a change.

I came away from the kibbutz with six months of Hebrew study, and, most importantly, with an expanded English vocabulary. I had wound up learning more English than Hebrew.

I decided to leave the kibbutz but remain in Israel, so I registered for another program. Before it began, I traveled back to Straubing to visit my family for a short time. I went to Natanya in Israel to study at the Olpan Akiva for six months. *Olpan* means language school in Hebrew.

This new program meant that I studied eight hours of Hebrew a day, six days a week. The school was language based and also taught folk music, dancing, and culture, and everyone from youngsters to the elderly studied there. When this program ended, I was very fluent in Hebrew, and was a well-rounded student and participant in Israeli culture.

I was now two or three months shy of my eighteenth birthday. I wanted to work in Israel and join the Israeli Army, but I was ineligible to serve because I was not a citizen. Since I was fluent in German, English, Yiddish, and Hebrew, I was marketable to become a tour guide, which I did not want to do, or work in a hotel, which was very appealing to me. I applied for a job as a receptionist at a hotel in Tel Aviv, but was told to come back when I was eighteen. The position would be held for me.

Waiting for time to pass until I turned eighteen, and with no money and no income, I decided to visit my parents in Germany. This time, they begged me not to return to Israel because they were afraid of terrorist attacks. At the same time, they respected the fact that I did not wish to live in Germany, so they offered a compromise.

"Why not go to the United States?" they suggested. "We understand that you don't want to live in Germany, but maybe there's a safer place than Israel."

Another chapter of my life began with those words.

CHAPTER 9
A New Life in America

ON THE ONE HAND, I was a rebellious and independent teenager, very different from my siblings. But on the other hand, I was an obedient daughter and required my parents' financial and emotional support. I loved my parents and didn't want to go against them. But I hated living in Germany. As terrorist attacks in Israel increased, so did my parents' anxieties about me staying there. During my return visit from Israel, my father approached me with a beseeching look.

"Your mother and I get it now—you really don't want to stay in Germany," he said. "But we are so very worried."

The agony in his eyes convinced me, and I gave in. My father handed me some money and said, "Spend a few months in America, and see if you like it."

Since I had no job and no income, I decided to follow their wishes and travel to the United States.

One young man I looked up turned out to be the man I would marry. My future husband, and I had met in Israel, and now he lived in Spring Valley in Rockland County, New York. I flew from Munich and stayed with my cousins, Roberta and Alex, out on Staten Island. It turned out that most of the people from the kibbutz lived in California, and traveling to see them was too complicated and expensive. I spent my time in New York, and since I wasn't doing anything of note, I started dating Jay.

He had been born in Israel and was also a child of Holocaust survivors. He was twenty-six, and I was a very young seventeen. It was not love at first sight, but we had something very much in common: the need to make our parents happy. Here we had the Yiddish-speaking Jewish girl matched with the Jewish boy living in America with his parents, whose backgrounds were similar to that of the girl's father. In the eyes of our parents, this was a recipe for a perfect marriage.

A few months following my eighteenth birthday, Jay and I decided to get married and settle down in Spring Valley. Now my parents could sleep well at night. I was out of Israel, and there would be no more worries about my safety.

Putting my dad's happiness before mine was second nature to me by now. I was convinced that marrying a Jew and moving to the United States would ease his pain. After spending two years learning Hebrew, I now had to learn American English, which was different from the English I had learned in school. I had to adapt to another new culture very different from ones I had grown accustomed to. Living in the suburbs meant driving everywhere. Nothing could be done on foot. The phrase "around the corner" could mean twenty minutes in the car.

I missed the street cafés, the fresh markets, and the public transportation. Unannounced visits to someone's home were a no-no. And nobody had heard of goose down blankets. The move to America was not easy, and I cried many times. But I couldn't take the chance of hurting my dad, so I didn't tell him.

The Holocaust deeply affected Jay's parents, but very differently from mine. His seemed very bitter, and this may have had an impact on his upbringing, which I received a taste of in the beginning of our marriage. Jay was often negative and didn't allow himself to have much joy in life.

While I was attending second-generation support groups, I learned that in an effort to quickly rebuild a family life, many survivors rushed into loveless marriages. These children were often raised in an unhappy home and as a result were unable to develop a positive self- image. My father was the opposite: he wanted me to be happy and embrace life. After a while, I no longer wanted to be pulled into Jay's world of sadness. But because of our two children, I hung in there as long as possible.

What we really had in common were our parents. Since both of his were survivors and so was my father, my first husband and I had a certain kinship. His mother and father were like another set of parents to me. We both felt responsible for making our parents happy.

In the end, we were living together like brother and sister. We went to temple every Friday for services because we knew it pleased our parents. Pleasing our parents was the focus of our marriage.

My mother had concerns right from the start. She saw the differences in our upbringing and attempted to point them out to me, and warned me on the day of my wedding not to marry him.

I thought I knew everything.

My mother begged, "Please come back home with me. Please don't marry him."

She had very good instincts, and it turned out that she was 100 percent correct. But I didn't want to go back to Germany, and I was tired of traveling.

I finally ended the marriage after ten long years.

CHAPTER 10
Another Beginning

MY DIVORCE TOOK A TOLL ON MY MENTAL AND PHYSICAL WELL-BEING. My parents and siblings decided that it would be best for me and my two children, Danny and Rebecca, to temporarily return to Germany. After a decade of living away from my hometown, it felt great to be back and spend time with my family. My parents and siblings were loving and caring, and tried to help me get through this very tough period in my life.

What was to become of me? Where would I live?

My family thought it would be best for me, as a single mother, to stay in Germany. I would have support and backup when needed. I must admit, the offer sounded very attractive—raising my children with the loving support of my family. How could I resist?

People get divorced all the time, but in my case it became so much more complicated. Where was I supposed to live? How could I return to Germany after all this time? I would always be a Jew in Germany, never a German Jew. Did I want my children to feel the way I felt growing up?

My children were born in America. They were Americans, and I needed to bring them home.

The three of us returned to New York. One year had passed, and life was starting to pick up. I had a part-time job as a medical assistant. As soon as my children were a little older, I planned on returning to school. As a single mother, I didn't think I would be very successful in the dating world, so I pretty much kept to myself on my days off. I was twenty-nine.

But a night out changed my plans, and my life.

One winter evening, I was to pick up my girlfriend from her waitressing job. She was running late and asked me to have a seat at the bar. I ordered a drink. While waiting for her, I looked over to my left and noticed a young man having a beer and reading the newspaper. He was clearly focused on the article he was reading. Curious, I took a glance at the paper, thinking he wouldn't notice. He was reading about the first war in Iraq. Just as I was about to move a bit closer to see the end of the article, he turned to me.

"Please help yourself," he said kindly. "I am done reading."

A bit embarrassed, I took the paper and thanked him. My girlfriend came by and said that she was going to have to work a bit later. The young man turned to me again and asked, "I hear an accent. Where are you from?"

"Germany," I replied.

"Oh," he said. "My name is Jon, nice to meet you. I wrote my thesis about the German resistance."

I felt resentful. Was he some kind of German sympathizer? I replied, "Well, it had to have been a short thesis, since there was not much of it. And Claus Von Stauffenberg miserably failed to assassinate Adolph Hitler." I was getting heated and ready for an argument. "I am German, and Jewish," I informed him.

He started laughing and said, "I am Jewish, too. My full name is Jonathan."

I forgot about my girlfriend. Jon and I talked about World War II history all evening. This man at the bar turned out to be the love of my life.

Jon and I married eight months after we met.

Passover was my first occasion to meet Jon's entire family. I remember walking up the stairs in the home of his parents, Gil and Lenore, and seeing so many relatives. Uncles, aunts, cousins, and grandmothers were gathered around the table getting ready for the Seder. This was a group of laughing, smiling people having a great time and sharing stories at the dinner table. Aunt Shelly talked about her work, cousin Lance spoke about his college experiences, and Adam was preparing for his new job.

Gatherings in my house back in Germany had been a bit different. Sitting around the holiday table were my parents, siblings, and sometimes members of the temple. The talk would be: Uncle Jacob died in Auschwitz, Cousin Rifka was gassed in Treblinka, and Uncle Moshe had survived Buchenwald.

I sometimes envy Jon's upbringing. He was able to enjoy his childhood without strings attached. He had many friends, and was allowed to participate in sleepovers and after-school activities. He enjoyed baseball and playing in bands. In my eyes, Jon was the all-American boy. While he was living his teen years to the fullest, I was in Tel Aviv demonstrating against a concert featuring the music of Richard Wagner, an anti-Semitic German composer, and one of Hitler's favorites.

Jon is a gentle soul who has managed to calm my temper over the years. He taught me not to be out for the kill when arguing with someone. Going for the kill was my way of letting out anger, which I felt was caused by the Jews walking into the gas chambers so passively.

Becoming part of Jon's family was like a treasure to me. Finally, there was some normalcy in my life. Jon legally adopted my two children. He took care of them from the minute he met them.

Alexander Robert, our son, who is named after Alexander the Great and an uncle of my mother-in-law, followed soon after we married.

I thought of my father and his family as my sons were bar mitzvahed when they turned thirteen. Not long after my father's bar mitzvah ceremony, he was sent to the ghetto in Poland. This is what I often thought about, and it was difficult for me to look at my sons when they were the same age. When my father was sixteen, he was imprisoned in Auschwitz. If my sons acted up, I reminded them that at the same point in his life, their grandfather was in a concentration camp. While it was upsetting to me, my words had little impact on my sons back then. They would look at me and say, "What are you worried about? There's no more Auschwitz."

They were right. These were my own anxieties, and I was projecting them onto my boys. But I couldn't help it. When I thought of my father and what he had endured, all of a sudden our problems meant nothing. God only knows what he had to do to survive. It was by pure luck that he made it out alive. He had been capable of working, and I remember him saying that the ones who went in skinny were the tougher ones in the camps.

When my first child, Danny, turned thirteen, this triggered something in me. I began thinking more and more about the Holocaust, genocide, and the Germans who sent innocent children to the gas chambers. I became aware of the misery of children all over the world, the cruelty and inhumanity of people, how families were ripped apart, and the psychological impact it had on the survivors and their children. And when I became more aware of what my father had gone through, I became anxious, very anxious. This anxiety was passed on to my kids.

Like my father, I continually worried that something could happen to my children, so I hated the thought of leaving them with a babysitter, at a day-care center, or sending them to camp. I wasn't alone. Many second-generation survivors have had this same experience. Instead of encouraging our kids to be independent, we wanted them by our side. When my son was in nursery school, I could hardly leave the driveway of the school after I dropped him off. I would be sitting there, panicking that something would happen. Eventually I had to leave, but I thought of him during the day and worried each time my telephone would ring.

I never let my children stand at the bus stop alone; I was afraid that someone would grab them. My kids were not permitted to attend sleepovers at the homes of friends. People had different rules in their homes, and I was worried about child molestation. You don't know who is in the home.

My three children had a midnight curfew. "If you're not in the door by then, I'm coming to pick you up," I told them, and meant it.

I remember the first time I sent my kids to day camp. I had a very hard time putting them on the bus. I finally summoned up the courage to do so, but then I followed the bus for the first few days to make sure it went into the camp. It's a little crazy, I know. But I was so worried that they could be standing somewhere, lost. I couldn't even enjoy the day. I sat home chewing my fingernails and worrying. They must have been six and eight years of age. This hovering over my children and the nurturing are all part of being a second-generation survivor.

I did work my way through most of my anxieties. I was aware of them, which is a great first step, and I wanted normalcy for my children and for me. I started seeing a therapist, who helped me through them. I also attended Holocaust support groups and found that others had the same anxieties. I found it very helpful to know that I was not alone in this behavior. Our parents were scared that something would happen to us. They lived in fear, and so do we. We were encouraged to educate ourselves and not to take risks that might endanger us.

Some of my father's fears have manifested themselves into anxieties and phobias. I still have some, and I feel that they are because of the Holocaust. Because I am extremely claustrophobic, I am unable to use elevators and must take the stairs. This has prevented me from attending some social functions. This may be traced back to the cramped and squalid conditions with little air inside the cattle cars used to transport Jews to concentration camps. I am afraid that I will be trapped inside an elevator.

While I am petrified of flying, I do travel to Germany once a year to visit my father. But my flying is limited to visiting him. I don't have fear about the airplane crashing, but being trapped inside that small space is terrifying.

My brothers and sister have similar phobias. My brother, for example, is unable to drive over bridges. He will do whatever he can to detour, even driving hundreds of miles out of his way to avoid them.

My three children were sent to Hebrew school, just like I was, and I began educating them about the Holocaust then. It seemed like the most appropriate time, after a letter was sent home requesting permission for the school to discuss it. My children knew about the Holocaust, but they didn't ask too many questions. As with many young people, when you mention grandparents, they think they lived in ancient history. They are so far removed from the Holocaust, Germany, and my father, but I did explain to my kids that they are the grandchildren of a survivor.

"My father survived by miracles, and you are here for a reason," I said to them.

As they got a bit older, they showed more interest. I told them about how my father would see Josef Mengele on the ramp at Auschwitz; their mouths dropped open and they were wide-eyed.

They could not believe the horror. Danny, who was sixteen at the time, understood more about the Holocaust when we saw the movies *Schindler's List* and *The Pianist*. The director of *The Pianist*, Roman Polanski, is a survivor from Poland, and his film tells the tale of one normal family whose lives were destroyed by the Nazis. My son started asking me questions about my family after this movie, so I was thankful that it provoked his interest.

But *The Pianist* is the last Holocaust movie I will ever see. I can no longer handle the subject anymore in films. It's much too upsetting. The family in the movie reminded me of my father's. The sister of the pianist looked very much like the photograph of my father's sister. It was too depressing and left me distraught for days. My father never saw it.

When we went to Germany and visited my father in 2010, I took Alex to the Dachau concentration camp. "What is this?" he asked while standing near the crematoriums. "Is this made for tourists?" He became upset. "This area is filled with flowers, bushes, park benches, and this little wooden bridge crossing over a stream. It looks like a place to have a picnic. Why would you beautify something that was so unimaginably horrific? Hmm", he said scratching his head. "But you never know." Did the Germans at that time with their twisted minds force Jews to decorate their own fate?" I still remember Alex's perplexed look as we left Dachau.

CHAPTER 11
A Love Story Ends

MY MOTHER WAS DIAGNOSED WITH PANCREATIC CANCER IN JANUARY 1999. I remembered her visiting us the summer before, just after we had installed a pool in the backyard of our home. She was sixty-six years old and wearing a bikini, and she looked better than I did.

That December, she took my father to his doctor for a regular checkup. His health was fine, but she complained of being always very tired, so the doctor ran some blood tests. He referred her to a hematologist. We were so naïve; we never thought it could be cancer. That word was not used in our house. The doctor said he needed to take a bone marrow sample and sent her for sonograms. She needed surgery.

The telephone rang a few days after. It was my sister.

"Listen, you have to sit down. I have to tell you something," Hannah said.

These words left me very worried, and I sat down on a chair in my kitchen.

"I just spoke with the surgeon," she said. "It's Mom. When they opened her, they found that the cancer had metastasized to her liver and spleen as well. She has nine months to live."

My beautiful mother...I couldn't believe it. I was immediately in denial. It had never occurred to me that my mother might die.

"They're all wrong!" I cried. "This isn't happening."

I often wondered what took me so long during her illness to comprehend that she was seriously ill and her life was ending. One could say that it was denial. But I am not so convinced. Most people my age experience aging, death, long illnesses, and hospital visits through their grandparents, uncles, or aunts. Most of my relatives were murdered. For me, there was no prelude to dealing with death.

Nine months to live. It couldn't be. I ran into the garage, got in my car, drove down the street a ways from the house, parked, and screamed. I didn't want my children to hear the sounds that came out of me—sounds I had thought only animals could make.

I thought about talks with my mother, who typically gave excellent advice and wisdom.

She said, "Don't be so quick to go with the boys. They love to talk about it, and they will talk behind your back. You'll be the talk of the town and get a bad reputation." She was always concerned with the reputations of her daughters.

"Try not to get sick and complain too much" she often said while talking about men. It doesn't interest them."

She gave me hints about life. "Love and hate are very close."

When my first husband and I divorced, she asked me, "Do you love him?"

"I hate him," I replied. "I hate being with him."

"You have to be numb," she said. "And then you know it's over."

She also advised me, "It's up to a woman to keep harmony in the house. You need time for yourself and for your husband. It's important that children have a schedule. You cannot be friends with your children. Friends, they make in school. They need a father and a mother. Most of all, do not be friends with your teenagers. They need to know someone is in charge."

Sometimes she embarrassed me with her wisdom. "Let me explain the life cycle of a guy," she said. "In his twenties and thirties, he likes to have good sex and lots of it. In his forties and fifties, he may prefer a good meal."

She taught me the difference between a husband and wife if one is having an affair. "A man who cheats on his wife brings her flowers to deal with the guilt," she said. "The wife? After her affair, she takes a shower."

I traveled to Straubing at Passover and stayed with her during chemotherapy. Pancreatic cancer is one of the deadliest forms, and the chemotherapy just doesn't work. I was in such denial that I didn't think she would die. My sister took her to chemotherapy to spare my father. And there were no nurses in the house; it was Hannah who took care of Mom during her illness.

My mother was a very, very strong woman, and the entire time she was sick, she only said, "I am seriously ill." She never said *cancer*, and she never said that she was dying.

I remember her standing in the kitchen. She had lost so much weight, and it seemed as if she had aged by thirty years overnight. She looked like she was ninety years old. Her personality had changed, too, and she had become more withdrawn. She didn't leave the house after her surgery. She never really recovered from that, and returned to the hospital after suffering an embolism. She was in a great deal of pain. This wasn't my mother anymore.

After I returned to New York, Jon and I decided to visit again during August and booked our flights. A few days before we were scheduled to leave, my sister telephoned me at six in the morning. I knew this couldn't be a good call.

"I just spoke to the doctor," Hannah said quietly. "Can you come today or tomorrow? It would be a really good idea. And tell Jon to bring a suit."

Immediately, I telephoned the airline and asked, "By any chance, do you have two seats to Munich for today?"

We booked them, and by noon we were on our way to the airport. With the time difference, we landed at eight in the morning. We drove as quickly as we could to the family house. My sister said that my mother kept asking for me and that she held on, knowing I was on my way.

My mother and I talked that morning as I sat with her. She was on her deathbed, but she recognized that I was there.

We were all so worried about my father, thinking he might die of a broken heart. The entire family was there, including my mother's daughter from her first relationship. Mom lay in the arms of my sister and me, and I held her tightly from both sides. My father stood behind us, and I kept checking to see that he hadn't dropped dead of a heart attack. He was very quiet as he tried to keep himself together. They had been with each other for fifty years.

My mother died almost exactly nine months after she was diagnosed, in 1999. We knew, of course, that she wanted a Jewish burial.

But the rabbi informed Hannah and me, "There's a problem. Only a Jewish woman can prepare her body for burial, and the woman who normally handles this is ill. You have to do it yourselves."

I thought I was going to pass out.

"You don't have to fear the dead," the rabbi assured us. "You have to fear the living. You have to do it. Meet me in the morgue."

I began to cry. I could not do this.

My sister, the strong one, was going to go ahead because it had to be done.

"Don't leave me alone," Hannah said. "I cannot do this myself."

I pulled myself together. This was what our mother wanted.

When we arrived at the morgue, a drawer was open and there was her body.

My claustrophobia kicked in, and I wondered, *What if she is still alive?*

I was petrified. But our mother needed to be treated with respect and dignity, even in death, and we were going to give her a proper burial. I wasn't going to let my sister down. Hannah and I stood in the morgue shaking like leaves. We were handed gloves and a bucket by the rabbi.

"Let's begin," he said.

I took a deep breath. We entered the room where our mother's body lay. I glanced carefully over to the table. She looked calm and peaceful, and she was still beautiful, even in death. All my fears disappeared, and I began to follow the rabbi's sacred instructions.

We followed Jewish law, and undressed her and washed her body using a sponge and a bucket of water. The instructions were specific, bathing from head to toe. The rabbi purified her body by pouring water over her in an uninterrupted flow. He showed us how to wrap her body in a shroud, which was made in Israel. The shroud, called a *tachrichim*, symbolizes that in the eyes of God, all of us are equal. The rabbi then said a prayer. When she was fully prepared and dressed, we lifted her into a plain wooden casket. According to Jewish tradition, her body was not to be left alone prior to burial, so the rabbi or Hannah and I were with her.

I am proud to have given our mother a proper Jewish burial. It gave me closure. Had we been in the United States, we would have had more options, with more Jewish women available to help. But we were in Straubing, and there were no volunteers for this job.

My mother was buried on August 18, 1999, on my parents' wedding day. They had been together for fifty loving years.

My father cried; he was inconsolable. This woman who loved and nurtured him, who converted to Judaism for him, who gave him four children, who carried on the Jewish traditions for him, was gone forever.

We sat *shivah* (a weeklong mourning period) in the house, but kept it private with only immediate family. It was therapeutic to be there together to mourn my mother. We spoke about good times, and once in a while the not-so-good times, as happens in every family. We were talking about my mother and trying to say only positive things, until someone made a somewhat negative comment about her being too hard on us at times.

My father remarked, "You are supposed to say the truth about the dead. You take the good with the bad. You're not supposed to sugarcoat anything."

This is what I love about my father—very pragmatic, understanding and realistic, loving and kind.

The loss of my mother was very painful, and I miss her terribly. I often quote her. She was a wise woman with great instincts, and I wish that I could tell her that she was right about everything she told me. A day doesn't go by without me saying, "My mother said" this or that.

There is a physical resemblance, and I share some personality traits with my mother. Personality-wise, I have a softer, more sensitive side. My mother was tougher than I am. She was also more consistent.

She had a very old-fashioned side, yet she had an illegitimate child. She never got over it and tried to live it down, but it was like wearing a scarlet letter. Her family had shunned her; she had no one to turn to and was all alone in the world. She worked long hours to earn money to support her child. After my mother married and was busy raising the four of us, our half sister, Petra, came to live with us for a short time. She had been raised by our mother's good friend and was twelve or thirteen when she decided that she wanted to come live with us. This did not work out. She was resentful and could not get over my mother having given her up. Too much time had gone by, and she couldn't bond with us. When she eventually left to be with her future husband, she cut off all contact with us.

Petra has been married to the same man for over thirty-five years, and they have two children. They live a few hours from Straubing, and she visited my mother while she was ill. She attended the funeral, but we've since lost contact with her again.

Hannah tends to our mother's grave in Straubing at least once a week. When I travel to Germany and visit my sister, we tend to the grave, and I put a rock on top of the headstone. Even when I'm not at the cemetery, my mother is with me, every single day. There are photographs of her all over my house and my father's home. We have family photographs everywhere, but the ones that are missing—and are missed—are the ones of my father's family members who were murdered during the Holocaust.

My mother 1 year before she died in 1998.

My Dad 1998

My siblings and I in Straubing in 2011.

CHAPTER 12
Three Generations

AS A SECOND-GENERATION SURVIVOR, not only am I deeply affected by issues of anti-Semitism, but I also feel that I am being held hostage by the Holocaust.

One thing I never do is complete census forms. I leave this to my husband. There are so many questions, and it becomes overwhelming.

Are you black? Are you white?

I'm scared. In my mind, I think back to the Nazis going door-to-door in Germany compiling information about the Jews and using it against them. I know it's different here, but I cannot help but imagine what life was like then and the fear that people had.

Here in the United States, when people talk about their college years and the friends they made, I feel like an outsider. I didn't attend college; I lived on a kibbutz and then got married.

Cautiousness about life has been transferred to my children, who have similar phobias and anxieties. Two of my children are married, and they live ten minutes from my home. They don't like being apart from me. My sister's children live within ten minutes' walking distance of her home, and her son and daughter live in same apartment building. Almost every weekend, my two brothers and their families travel to Straubing to see our father and sister and her family.

Like me, my daughter doesn't like to travel much or fly. My younger son hates changes and enjoys his routines. My older son is very introverted.

I hope to someday rid myself of my elevator phobia. Elevator rides feel like torture. I'm afraid that I will get stuck, so I walk up and down the stairs rather than get in one. My anxieties kicked in after I had my children.

I can trace these issues back to how I was raised as the daughter of a Holocaust survivor. Just as my parents could not encourage their children to go out and take risks, I could not do so either.

My older son works for my husband in his business, while my daughter is a special education teacher in the local public schools. My younger son, a senior in high school, wants to study art in college.

I have mixed feelings about Alex going off to school. We have a very close family, and I'm not sure how I will feel if he is not here.

My father and sister are the ones who continue the Jewish tradition and keep it alive in our family. My father is president of the Straubing Synagogue and attends services every Friday and Saturday. There are more than eight hundred members, and he is the driving force that keeps it going. Most of the Jews there now are Russians, and you would think you were in a synagogue in Moscow. My father raised close to a million German marks to restore the synagogue in1988; it was crumbling and badly in need of repair. I flew over for the unveiling the following year and was there at the ceremony when the German government honored my father.

Straubing Synagogue

Inside of Straubing Synagogue photographed from women's balcony

The unveiling of the Straubing synagogue was a very proud moment for my family. I will never forget standing on the balcony looking down at my father as he stood so proud wearing his *tallit*, (prayer shawl) standing behind the *bimah* (reading stand) while he gave a speech. In the audience, there were several prominent German politicians, like the minister of state, Alfred Dick; the senior mayor, Ludwig Scherl; and the senator of the Central Council of Jews in Germany, Julius Spokojny. A special cantor from Berlin was hired to perform El Malei Rachamim, the prayer of remembrance, to honor the six million Jews that had perished. The soulful chanting of the cantor triggered a memory of a story my mother once told me. During *Kristallnacht*, (The Night of Broken Glass) in November 1938, a mob of locals stormed into the synagogue with gasoline canisters in an attempt to burn it down.

Before they were able to do this, someone from the fire department warned them that if they set the synagogue on fire, the entire neighborhood would go up in flames. Instead they decided to destroy the interior of the building and whatever was inside. The next day, the teachers of the school nearby led their classes to the vandalized synagogue. Some of the windows were still intact. The students were ordered to throw rocks through them. Twenty-two years later I started first grade in the very same school.

After the war, a man went to the police station with a big black box. Inside the box were the Torah rolls and candlesticks from our synagogue. It turned out that this man was a police officer and had hid them until the war ended. They are the only items that were not destroyed. My father used this story as an example when he used to tell us that there were also good Germans amongst the evil.

As president of the Straubing Synagogue, he has received many honors, including the Bundesverdienstkreuz, which is the order of merit from the Federal Republic of Germany. He goes to his office for two hours every day, answers questions, prepares for the holy days, and helps make funeral arrangements. He then returns to the family home where my sister dotes on him. He's a diabetic, so he is careful with his diet. When one of his grandchildren visits, and if he has enough energy, he'll take a short walk, sometimes wheeling his great-grandchild, Sophie. He watches World War II history programs and the news on television, listens to the news on the radio, and reads the newspaper every day. He knows more about the politics of the United States than most Americans, I think.

My mother used to light the Yarzheit candles. My sister does it now.

The Holocaust is always with me. I would like people to learn from history and to change from it.

We're in the age of bullying—on the Internet, in school, at home, and in the workplace. "Stand up for yourself," I insist. If you can get a bully to listen as you explain who you are and what you stand for, you have a much better chance of being heard and understood.

I learned to survive by standing up for myself as the only Jew in my school, and I gained respect this way. I am the daughter of two strong parents—one of whom survived eight concentration camps during the Holocaust, and the other a survivor of World War II, poverty, and isolation, and someone who was ostracized because she had a daughter out of wedlock.

I can adapt to anything and anyone. I am flexible in any situation. I can get along with Germans. I can think like they do, and recite quotes of famous German writers. I can also be Jewish, converse in Hebrew, and cook a Jewish meal. I can be black or white. I can be silent and I can be heard.

My philosophy is to do what you can to protect and help a weaker child or person; speaking up is better than being silent.

I remember speaking about my father's story of his survival during the Holocaust, and what it meant to me, with a group of high school students a few years ago. Once you start talking history, teenagers become bored. I know this from my own children. The past is of little interest to them. But when I spoke about bullying, they became very interested because it happens to so many.

"Be proud of who you are," I advised them.

One girl told me, "I'm from South Korea. People make fun of me and think I'm from North Korea."

I told her to bring a map and show others where she's from. That way, she would not be passive and could show others reality.

This isn't a perfect world—you can't always turn the other cheek. Educate and inform others as you judge the circumstances.

The Holocaust may have occurred over seventy years ago. But genocide is still happening around the world. The situation in Rwanda brought back memories of the Holocaust. In 1994, almost one million people were mass murdered in violence in a war between two rival ethnic factions, the Hutu and the Tutsi. This was a crime against humanity, eliminating people because of their race and religion. This was what the Nazis tried to do.

I wish the Americans had saved the Jews sooner. With Rwanda, then President Bill Clinton said how much he regretted that he didn't do as much as he could have.

Anti-Semitism and hatred against the Jews are still here today, and make me sick to my stomach. Mel Gibson was arrested for drunk driving in 1996 and told the arresting officer, "Fucking Jews...the Jews are responsible for all the wars in the world." Why was it necessary for him to blame Jews? And more recently, in 2011, British fashion designer John Galliano was found guilty in France of making anti-Semitic remarks. Someone had a video camera and captured his rant, in the event anyone has doubts about what he said. He had been drinking, and he said to a group of women in a Paris café, "I love Hitler... People like you would be dead. Your mothers, your forefathers would all be fucking gassed." He was head designer for Dior, and the company condemned him and fired him.

At the 2011 Cannes Film Festival, director Lars von Trier admitted that he was a Nazi and said, "I understand Hitler...I sympathize with him a bit." What can he possibly sympathize with after Hitler killed millions of people? But Von Trier did not stop there. "There was a point to this whole thing. I think history shows that we are all Nazis somewhere, and there are a lot of things that can be suddenly set free, and the mechanics behind this setting free is something we really should investigate, and the way we do not investigate it is to make it a taboo to talk about it," he said.

What did we do to deserve these comments?

It doesn't stop.

In 2011, vandals desecrated a monument to Jews in Jedwabne, a town in Poland, the country where my father was born. In July 1941, forty Poles rounded up all of the town's Jewish residents, forced them into a barn, locked the doors, and set it on fire. A monument was later erected to acknowledge the lives of the dead. Then cowards spray-painted a swastika, the initials SS, and the phrases "I don't apologize for Jedwabne" and "they were flammable."

I was shaken when I heard this, knowing that there are people in the world today who loathe Jews. They are still here.

So, what is the moral of the story? Although I didn't live through World War II, the dark shadow of the Holocaust hangs over my generation and my children's generation. Thirty-four years ago, I made a decision to leave the country I was born in because I couldn't comfortably live with the German culture. Imagine spending years admiring a writer whose stories you passionately read, or an actress whose films you loved, or a musician whose music you danced to, and then finding out that they were supporters of the murderers of millions of people. I often wondered, when I met older Germans, what roles they had played during the war. To this day, it is still difficult for me to look forward to anything; I'm always waiting for something to happen to the Jews again.

Moving to Israel was not the answer for me. Becoming an American was a privilege and needed to be earned. By the time I became a citizen, I had mastered the English language and learned about American history and culture. Americans are compassionate, friendly, and inquisitive—accepting of different cultures and religions, but also genuinely interested in them. They are part of a hardworking nation and eager to fulfill their dreams. With strong will and ambition, anything is possible. To me, America has been and always will be the land of opportunity.

Adolf Hitler affected generations of survivors. He was the evil of the century who murdered millions and left his scars on millions more. When I hear his name, I get chills down my spine. In the beginning, people did not take him seriously, not in Germany or in other countries, including the United States. Who could have possibly imagined what would follow?

To survive the Holocaust was pure luck, with no rhyme or reason. It was just luck that you were able to work harder than the next, or to live without food longer. Many of these survivors have lived with guilt.

We used to attend shul in Straubing on the Jewish holidays. I remember looking at each of the men and women and knowing their stories. In the corner, as always, stood Mrs. Bernstein. She wore a scarf covering most of her head, and she held a small prayer book. She whispered prayers quietly. This was a very familiar picture. Every holiday, Mrs. Bernstein stood in the same spot doing the exact same thing, never looking up at anyone. Sometimes I saw tears falling on her *Siddur*.

Many times, I asked my mother, "What's wrong with Mrs. Bernstein?"

"You are too young to understand," she would tell me.

Always the same answer.

Only years later, when I was much older, did my mother tell me that Mrs. Bernstein gave birth to an infant during the war. Along with many other Jews, she and her newborn were hiding from the Germans. The baby kept crying and the others were afraid that the crying would alert the Germans to their hiding place. Mrs. Bernstein had no choice: she was forced to suffocate her baby.

Mrs. Bernstein's story came back to haunt me many times after I became a mother myself. At times, while holding Danny in my arms, feeding or playing with him, I pictured Mrs. Bernstein huddled with many other Jews in a cold, dark basement hidden away from the Nazis. Holding her infant…trying to stop it from crying of hunger, but not having any milk to feed her baby… forced to do the unthinkable. I want to go back and stand in the corner of the synagogue and cry with Mrs. Bernstein.

I never saw Mrs. Bernstein smiling or talking, only standing and praying. Her husband, tormented by these memories, committed suicide by jumping out of a window many years later after I had left Germany.

I looked at all of them in the synagogue, and I could see the numbers tattooed on their left forearms.

I remember reading somewhere that Hitler wanted to attend art school but his application was rejected. I wonder, if the school had accepted him, how the world would have been different.

When people talk about the Holocaust today, I tell them, "You have read about it. I lived with a man who went through this."

It's hard to imagine the impact, the unimaginable and unspeakable horrors that people endured, how their nightmares tormented them, and how it has affected their families. It continues to pass itself on from generation to generation. My father wanted to remain a Jew in Germany to get back at Hitler, to show the Nazis and the world that a Jew could survive.

Germany was in shambles after the war. Its first priority was not concern for the mental health of the survivors. Many people could have benefited and lived more content lives if this issue had been addressed. It would have helped them more than the monetary restitution they eventually ended up receiving.

My father still lives in Straubing in the family home, surrounded by his memories. Hannah and her boyfriend live with my father, take care of his needs, and keep him alive. If it were not for my sister, I think my father would have died ten or fifteen years ago. She has devoted her life to caring for him. She worries more about him than she does her children. We all keep him going. Sometimes he has panic attacks, and I'm sure his time in the concentration camps has something to do with them.

My father, Israel Offman, serves as president of the Straubing Synagogue, raising money to keep it open and remodel it. Both he and the building stand as a historical testament to the survival of the Jewish people, and as a legacy of love between a Jewish survivor of the concentration camps and a German woman. More than eight hundred people are members of the Straubing Synagogue today.

If my sister did not take care of our father at home, he likely would be residing in a nursing home with Germans, some of them former Nazi sympathizers or others who turned their backs on the Jews. This, we could never allow.

My father, in spite of what happened during the Holocaust, was thankful for the goodness of the German people who nourished him back to health after his liberation. While always remembering the Holocaust and its burden, he moved his life forward. He lived after the Holocaust, and he lived with love and without hate.

He is now eighty-seven.

My father recently said, "Every book written about the Jewish faith gives us the feeling of a rebirth. It is the job of each generation to make sure the next generation remembers what happened. In our family, my daughter Naomi took over this responsibility. May the stories of those no longer with us not be forgotten."

CPSIA information can be obtained at www.ICGtesting.com
Printed in the USA
LVOW06s1827041213

363880LV00004B/746/P